How to Be Treated Like a High Roller

How to Be Treated Like a High Roller

...Even though you're not one

Making Casino Visits More Fun and More Profitable

by

Robert M. Renneisen

Foreword by

John Patrick
Professional Gambler

A Lyle Stuart Book
Published by Carol Publishing Group

A Lyle Stuart Book
Published by Carol Publishing Group

Lyle Stuart is a registered trademark of Carol Communications, Inc.

Editorial Offices: 600 Madison Avenue, New York, N.Y. 10022
Sales and Distribution Offices: 120 Enterprise Avenue, Secaucus, N.J. 07094
In Canada: Canadian Manda Group, One Atlantic Avenue, Suite 105, Toronto, Ontario M6K 3E7

Queries regarding rights and permissions should be addressed to Carol Publishing Group, 600 Madison Avenue, New York, N.Y. 10022

Carol Publishing Group books are available at special discounts for bulk purchases, sales promotions, fund raising, or educational purposes. Special editions can be created to specifications. For details contact: Special Sales Department, Carol Publishing Group, 120 Enterprise Avenue, Secaucus, N.J. 07094

Manufactured in the United States of America
10 9 8 7 6 5 4 3 2 1

Library of Congress Cataloging-in-Publication Data
Renneisen, Robert
    How to be treated like a high roller, even though you're not / by Robert Renneisen : introduction by John Patrick.
        p. cm.
    "A Lyle Stuart book."
    ISBN 8-8184-0580-5
        1. Gambling. 2. Casinos. 3. Package tours. I. Title.
GV1301.R44   1992
795—dc20   91-45685
                                                    CIP

Contents

How to Be Treated Like a High Roller

Foreword

If you are glancing through this book, wondering if it is worth the price, believe me, it is. It's obvious you're interested in gambling or else you wouldn't be wasting your time peeking at a book on the subject, unless you had an urge to broaden your outlook on the art of casino life.

This book talks about the life of gambling. Not from a sense of how to play, but rather from a look at the other side of the table. The behind-the-scene moves that you, the player, only think about. It shows you how to acquire the comps that naturally tickle your appetite.

I've been gambling since New York was a prairie, so the players' side of the game was always easy to understand. In fact, most of you know the ins and outs of every casino game and how to play, but there is another side of casino life that you may not know, and it is covered in this book.

Several months ago, Bob Renneisen, the president of Claridge Casino Hotel in Atlantic City, mentioned that every time he gave a lecture, or went to dinner, or even walked through the casino, the patrons asked him about comps, ratings, perks, and all the other unknown facts about casino doings.

Most of these people couldn't understand the reasons why they weren't comped every time they walked into a casino. He decided to put together information that would help explain casino life from the other side of the table. I also have acquaintances who wouldn't know their elbow from a doorknob once they reach a table.

My friend I. M. Madork is a casual gambler who goes to the casinos maybe once a month and brings everything he can scrape together for a day at the tables. Last week, he went to battle with a handful of quarters, a couple of five dollar bills, three rolls of nickels, an Indian head penny, six canceled stamps and an I.O.U. for $6.67 that he'd been carrying in his back pocket from the last Friday night poker game he played in.

He picked a blackjack table as his initial point of attack. Madork bought in, played six hands, and spotted a casino floor person about twenty feet away.

"Excuse me...sir. Sir, excuse me...Yes, you. Will you come here please!!" It was a demand, not a request. The floor person came to Madork's table and inquired as to what the problem was.

Madork proceeded to ask for a comp dinner, due to the fact that he was a player who was out $18 and figured the casino had a moral obligation to buy him a meal as a reward for his giving them an opportunity to beat him.

"Hey, Mack, how you get a comp around here!!" Again, it was a demand, not a question. The floor person tried to explain the method by which players are rated at the tables, but Madork, who is living, breathing proof that there are such dorks in this world, would accept none of the explanations. He grabbed the remains of his buy-in and stormed off, cursing and yelling about the rotten treatment he had received.

Naturally, by the time he had retold his tale to fifty other people, the story had multiplied a hundred-fold. The casino gets a bad name and in fact the whole industry gets blasted by a ding-dong who thinks he deserves special treatment just because he climbs on a stool and plunks down a $5 bet.

Think about it. How many times have you had the same thoughts as I. M., without fully realizing the intricate guidelines by which these floor people are governed?

Rob Renneisen decided to elaborate on the unknown factors that the patrons could not possibly be aware of. He jotted down the things that occur behind the tables, putting you in the position of looking out across the table at the players. Most of all, he gives you insight into acquiring the extras that are there for you.

Bob put these things into book form and asked me if I thought there might be some interest from the public. Halfway through his writings I could see that there were things that even a veteran casino player would find enlightening. Even with thirty years of table play etched deep into my experiences, I'm almost ashamed to admit that there were some interesting rating procedures I wasn't even aware of. These are things that every casino player should know and can use all the time.

For that reason, I want to heartily endorse this book. If you go to the casinos and wish to get a sensible shot at winning, it's imperative that you know everything there is to know about both sides of the table.

My friend Lotta Kash goes to the tables with a lot of cash but doesn't know to get rated. Bob shows you how to utilize the thinking of the casinos and make them notice your play without your having to wear a bikini or an orange suit to get them to observe your bets and comp you.

Lotta Kash should be taken care of, but she's surrounded by other high rollers and gets lost in the crowd.

There are plenty of you who are frequent visitors to the gambling cities but who still haven't zeroed in on one casino.

Thereby you don't get the privilege of having a casino "adopt" you and reward your play.

All of these things are important if you hope to be comped. And since the casinos will take care of steady players, you should learn how to take advantage of these situations. This book shows you how.

A word or two on the author is in order and imperative if you have any doubt as to the validity of this information.

Rob Renneisen has been in the casino business for years, both in Atlantic City and Las Vegas and also in the Caribbean. The fact that he is president of a major hotel like the Claridge is living proof that he has paid his dues.

It takes a certain type of individual to make it to the top, especially since there are only a certain number of chairs and many, many candidates. You know that the president of a casino has danced a lot of dances, learned the ropes, and hung on to nail down one of only twelve available presidential positions in Atlantic City.

Bob Renneisen knows the casino business from both sides of the table and has the knowledge to be able to pass it along to the public so it could be taught how to take advantage of every offer.

His personal background is a study of experience and diversification. His dad was a colonel in the air force, so traveling around the country was old hat to him before he even got out of school.

That led him into the world of journalism, where he became a sports writer and even traveled with a major league team. In fact, his stories about some of the star players would fill another book, if he ever decided to lean in that direction.

In the late '60s, Bob entered the army where he was an infantry captain in Vietnam. After completing his tour of duty, he entered the business world and started the climb to his present position.

A tremendous speaker, Bob can hold an audience for hours with stories of casino life and behind-the-scene anecdotes. He has appeared on many live call-in TV shows and the candor he displays when answering with his callers is evident in this book.

Bob's lofty achievements at such an early age have made him outgoing and fully confident about his future. It's not unusual to see him stand and chat with players on the floor of the Claridge for long periods of time.

Bob has two children, Michele and Brian, and currently resides in South Jersey with his beautiful wife, Susan.

To sum up, Bob Renneisen is more than qualified as the author of this much needed book. I know you'll enjoy its style as well as its content. I found *How to Be Treated Like a High Roller* informative, easy to read, and the analogies of the different situations very entertaining. I'm sure you'll enjoy this book as much as I did.

John Patrick

Introduction

A fellow I once worked with used to have a little sign on his desk which read, "Please don't tell my mother I work in a casino. She thinks I play the piano in a whorehouse."

Mom didn't raise me to be a casino executive and I didn't plan on it either. It just happened by accident; but it was a lucky accident. I love my work and meet some of the most wonderful people imaginable—customers and co-workers alike. I met my beautiful wife working in a casino and, later, when we were married, we had our wedding reception in—you guessed it—a casino.

A lot has been written about casinos and gambling in general—much of it by individuals who aren't part of the casino business but are on the outside looking in. Those of us in the business often have a different perspective developed and shaped by our daily experience in casinos. Believe me, this experience is valuable.

Even though what you'll read in these pages is full of my own personal viewpoints, what I've written is based on what I've learned on the job in real casinos—not through books or personal interviews. I've worked as a vice president and senior vice president at casinos in Las Vegas, Atlantic City, and the Caribbean. At the time of this writing, I am the president of the Claridge Casino Hotel in Atlantic City.

I don't mean to imply that I'm the brightest guy around or the best casino executive to come down the pike. I learn daily from others who are better and brighter. However, I have worked many years in casinos—certainly enough time to be credible—and some of what I've learned may be useful to you on your future casino forays.

As part of my job, every day I answer questions from dozens of people who, perhaps like you, want to know all sorts of things about casinos. Things like…

> "How can I get a comp for lunch?"
> "How much should I tip the dealer?"
> "Why don't you have any $2 blackjack tables?"
> "How do I open a credit line?"
> "Has this machine *ever* paid a jackpot?"
> "Who's in charge?"
> "Where's the ladies room, please?"
> "I missed the bus back to Newark…"

A friend of mine, John Patrick, is a well-known professional gambler and author who has a TV show about casino games. Every now and then, as a guest on his show, I get questions from people who call in to ask about casino gambling. One night after a show, I remarked to John about how many people have the same questions.

"Why don't you write a book," John said. "If I can do it, so can you. Answer all those common questions and give people some insight about what goes on behind the tables. Tell a few funny stories, too."

So here's the book. I hope you find it helpful and entertaining. I've enjoyed writing it and, gratefully, received a lot of help and advice from my friends and co-workers in the casino business.

If you haven't guessed, I enjoy this business and can't think of anything else I'd rather do to earn a living. Even Mom is happy. She loves to play blackjack at a $5 table and, just like everybody else's mom, she's glad to know "somebody upstairs" who can get her a comp for the Deli.

If you don't have a kid "upstairs," there are other ways to get a comp and a lot of fascinating things to learn that can make your casino visits more fun and more profitable.

Fair enough?

Read on...and good luck!

P.S.: One thing about the casino business is that it's pretty risky...not the most secure job in the world, if you know what I mean. So, if you like the book, tell your friends and neighbors...it never hurts to have a second trade to fall back on.

1

The World of Casinos

Exciting, confusing, intimidating, naughty

So, you want to be treated like a high roller, right?

To begin, let's take stock of your feelings and attitudes about gambling and casinos in general.

When you walk into a casino, do you get a special feeling of excitement—like when you were a kid and your folks took you to an amusement park?

I do. Even after the years I've spent working in casinos in Las Vegas, Atlantic City, and the Caribbean, I still get that same special feeling when I walk onto the casino floor. It's a feeling of money, action, fun, and unique excitement that sets the casino apart as a separate world from our everyday lives.

Each morning, I see this same excitement mirrored in the faces of our guests as they walk through the front door. Their expressions say, "Here I can experience a different way of life. I can escape for a day. It's exciting. All things are possible!"

On your next casino visit, before you rush off to find your favorite machine or a hot craps game, take a minute and really look around. Ask yourself, "Why am I here? What makes it so exciting?"

Is it the always-present chance of becoming a winner—maybe even a BIG winner?

Sure, that's part of it, a big part; but what about the sights and sounds and special feelings in a casino? You've walked onto a stage where a cast of hundreds is waiting to entertain you; and, best of all, you are part of the act—the star of the show—because if it weren't for you, the rest of us wouldn't be here.

How is the stage set in your favorite casino? Is it brightly lit and bustling with action? Are the lights dimmed dramatically with little spotlights casting their narrow beams down on every table giving a feeling of mystery and passion? Is it booming with excitement or smoldering with thinly veiled emotion?

Casino managers and special designers spend thousands of hours and millions of dollars trying to create their own special ambiance in an effort to offer their players a unique fantasy world.

Just as in the theater, lights, sets, props, and costumes are part of the casino business. Look at the various gaming tables. Are they covered with traditional green layouts? Maybe hot red or cool blue?

What about the actors on your favorite casino stage—the dealers? Are they decked out in classy tuxedo shirts and bow ties, cowboy vests, luau shirts, or sailor suits? How do the dealers act? Are they fun and friendly or are they smugly quiet, daring you to step up and take a shot?

How about the "bosses" behind the tables in the pits? Are they chatting with the players or standing with arms crossed trying hard to look like they just spent the last half hour kissing the Godfather's hand?

When you go to a casino, do you get a subtle feeling that you're getting away with something kind of naughty? You know it's legal and all that, but, still, is there a whisper of emotion that tells you you're stepping into a world that's just a little risqué? Isn't that secretly part of the appeal casinos have?

What about intimidation?

Are you comfortable stepping up to a table and plunking down your money with the rest of the players—people who "know a lot more about gambling" and would embarrass you if you made a mistake or ask a dumb question?

Intimidation is a big, BIG factor that prevents a lot of people from having a better time in casinos. If you're one of them, don't let intimidation deprive you of a great experience.

If you don't know how to play, pick up a book and find out. None of the table games is difficult and you don't have to be a rocket scientist to sit down and have some fun; and, believe it or not, nobody is going to think you're dumb if you ask a question. The guy sitting next to you probably has the same question but is too intimidated to ask it. Who cares? You came to play, didn't you?

Overcoming intimidation is another psychological appeal of casino gambling. ("Okay, today's gonna be the day I leave that favorite slot machine and finally give roulette a try!")

What is it about your favorite casino that appeals to you?

Different strokes for different folks, right? That's why you'll find differences among the casinos. We want to give you a choice. Of course all of us hope that our design, and our costumes, and our actors will be more appealing than the other casinos'. We want your business.

The operative word here is "business." Casinos are a business, just like any other. Instead of selling shoes or toothpaste, we sell a good time. Players pay for their good time with the money they lose. (Not everybody loses, of course, but let's face it right up front: most people do. If they didn't, there wouldn't be any casinos!)

The money won by the casino is our equivalent to gross sales in other businesses. Out of the money we win, we pay our employees, all of our expenses and, hopefully, make a fair profit for our company.

So even though we want your business—and are willing to pay for it with comps, promotions, discounts, junkets, etc.—we are still running a business. In other words, there are limits to what we'll do and there are good reasons for those limits. One of the aims of this little book is to explain those reasons and give you an understanding of how and why casinos run their business. This knowledge will make it easier for you to learn how to be treated like a high roller.

You see, even though casinos are profit-making businesses, we would soon be out of business if we lost sight of what makes it all work.

Quite simply, you come to a casino to have a great time; it's our business to make sure that you do.

If this isn't the feeling you get from your favorite casino, shop around. Maybe there's another one out there that might appeal to you a little more.

Little white jelly rolls

I'll never forget the first time I was in a casino.

It was in the mid-1950s and I was about ten or eleven. My father and mother took my kid brother and me with them to Las Vegas for vacation.

We stayed in a little motel on the Strip. Well, to a ten-year-old kid, Las Vegas didn't seem too exciting. My brother and I hung out at the pool and went to see a movie with my dad downtown.

Every night, a baby-sitter showed up and Mom and Dad went to the casinos.

After a few days, the word "casino" developed implications of epic proportions for me.

One night, no baby-sitter. We are going out to dinner with the folks at—a CASINO!

It was a huge, towering palace with more neon lights than I'd ever seen in one place. The excitement was growing.

In through the front doors we went. Sure enough, it sounded exciting. I could hear coins jingling in the slot machines (not that I knew what a slot machine was), and clicking, whirring, murmuring sounds that I've since come to love as a unique song that every casino seems to sing.

It was okay for kids to walk through the casino there, so we strolled past the tables and slots to the elevator, which took us up to the restaurant.

It was a Polynesian room filled with wonderful, exotic aromas. The waitresses were all dressed in Hawaiian hula skirts and were a great improvement over the baby-sitter back at the motel.

No sooner had we been seated than one of the hula girls brought us a little silver tray with four snow-white steaming rolls.

They looked like little jelly rolls that had been sprinkled with powdered sugar and grated coconut—sort of like little roll-shaped Hostess "Snowballs." I'd never seen anything that looked so delicious—no wonder the folks came here every night.

My brother Charley was about five years old and he couldn't wait to stuff one of those jelly rolls in his mouth.

But he looked kind of funny—chewing real hard and not smiling.

Finally, as Dad started to laugh, Charley took it out of his mouth and unrolled it.

It was a white washcloth steamed in perfumed water.

I've never since been to an Oriental restaurant where they serve hot towels without thinking of my brother trying to eat the little white jelly roll in Las Vegas. I've never lost the excitement I first felt when I walked into that casino either.

2

Who's the Boss, Boss?

In order to get treated like a high roller, you need to learn how casinos operate and who calls the shots.

Boss is a very popular word in casinos. We have more "bosses" than most businesses, and casino "bosses" tend to be bossier than normal bosses.

On top of that, casino employees seem to use the words boss and bosses more frequently than non-casino employees.

When I walk through the casino on a typical day, more employees are likely to say, "Hey, Boss," than, "Hi, Bob," or, "Hey, You!"

Sometimes it makes me feel like the warden in *Cool Hand Luke* ("Hey, Boss, here I am in the bushes...still shakin', Boss.")

So, of course, when bosses like me hear "boss, boss, boss" all day long, we naturally do our best to look and act like bosses. This makes it very difficult for people in the casino to figure out who the real boss is...who's a pit boss and who isn't...who's a big boss and who's a little boss. Sometimes it's all very confusing unless you know the pecking order.

The most common mistake players make is to assume that everyone in civilian clothes behind the tables in the pit is a pit boss. That's what you thought, right?

Wrong, Blackjack Breath! There's only one pit boss in each pit. He or she is *the* boss of *that* pit, get it?

Maybe the easiest way to sort it all out for you is to start from the top and go through a typical casino organization.

Vice President, Casino Operations

Usually, the senior executive with responsibility for the casino is a *vice president of casino operations*. In addition to being Numero Uno in the table games department, he or she may also be responsible for the casino hosts and casino credit departments and sometimes for slots as well.

The vice president normally reports to the president or an executive vice president. These are all major league bosses, in the full flower of casino bosshood, who earn their daily bread not in the casino, but in an office "upstairs" (even if "upstairs" isn't). This is why they have come to be known collectively as "the man upstairs."

Casino Manager

The real day-to-day boss of the casino is the *casino manager*. He or she is responsible for all table games, including scheduling, games procedures, table limits, personnel, and training.

While vice presidents sometimes are individuals who earned their spurs as bosses in other areas of the business, the casino manager nearly always comes up through the ranks, starting as a dealer. In other words, he knows his way around the casino and, usually, has the last word when a dispute or question arises.

Shift Bosses

Although the casino manager may have one or more assistant managers who fill in for him in his absence, the next management level is that of *casino shift manager*, also known as shift boss.

As their title implies, the shift managers are in charge of a casino shift—day shift, swing shift, or graveyard shift. While the casino manager may be tied up on administrative matters in his office, the shift boss will normally be found walking around the casino floor—looking and acting like the boss that he or she is.

As the senior casino executive on the floor, the shift boss, in many aspects, is the boss of the whole establishment on that shift. Shift bosses frequently are consulted about unusually large comps (limos or air travel, for instance) and often make decisions about which players can be comped into which guest rooms when the hotel is nearly full. This is why some casino-hotels refer to heavy occupancy periods as being on "shift manager's status." In other words, you don't get a room unless the shift manager approves it.

Whenever the casino is in operation, day or night, one of the shift bosses is there and in charge.

Pit Bosses

The gaming tables in casinos are normally arranged in open rectangles, ovals or similar groupings known as "pits." Sometimes a pit is comprised completely of similar games—all blackjack or all craps, for example. Often, however, a pit will have several types of games.

In each pit, one person is in charge—*the pit boss*, responsible for everything that goes on in his or her pit.

The pit boss's job includes many activities designed to protect the integrity and honesty of the games. Casinos establish various policies and procedures that employees and customers are required to follow. Pit bosses are experienced at recognizing deviations from these standard practices—deviations that sometimes call attention to a mistake or worse.

Every casino, for example, has certain procedures it requires its dealers to use when shuffling cards, when collecting or paying bets, when placing cards into the discard rack, etc. Most also have rules regarding how they want the players to act—how and when to place your bet, when to touch the cards or take the dice, and so forth.

The aim of these dozens of procedures on every game is to insure consistency of activity. In this way, something not in accordance with established procedures becomes easier for a supervisor or surveillance employee to detect. Pit bosses spend a great deal of time making sure the floor persons and dealers are politely enforcing these procedures in their pits.

In addition to procedural and integrity matters, the pit boss is responsible for insuring that there is an adequate number of gaming chips at each table, frequently calling for a "fill" if a table is losing and starts to run low.

Pit bosses also insure that dealers and floor persons in the pit are treating the players in accordance with the specific policies of the casino.

Some casinos, for example, discourage conversation between employees and players. (This is known in the business as "Dummy up and deal.") Others strive for a friendly, open atmosphere where dealers are free to chat with the customers and make them feel more comfortable in what can, to some people, be an intimidating environment. Whatever the casino's policy is, the pit boss is there to insure that it's followed.

Finally, the pit boss is most likely the one who will have final approval on comp decisions for players in that pit, basing the decision (hopefully) on the customer's gambling activity and the policies of the house.

Floor Persons

Floor persons are the frontline supervisors in a casino. In every pit, working for the pit boss, there are a number of floor persons, each of whom supervises several games.

The floor person is the one who closely monitors the action on each table. He or she enforces policies and procedures, verifies currency and chip transactions, monitors the buy-in amounts of players, and sees to their comfort and satisfaction. In the event of a mistake or dispute, the floor person takes appropriate corrective action.

In most casinos, the floor person is the individual to ask for a marker *if you already have established a line of credit* at the casino.

Player ratings are also the responsibility of the floor person. By keeping track of how much a player bets and for how long, a rating is established that, among other things, is useful to the pit boss in determining whether or not a comp is warranted.

Box Persons

The *box person* is a specialized supervisor responsible for one craps game. He or she is the one who sits on a low stool behind the gaming chips on the craps table. (We often refer to a box person's job as "sitting box.")

The box person is in charge of running that one dice table. He or she handles all currency and chip transactions, monitors and inspects the dice being used, supervises bet payoffs, and generally controls the game.

Dealers

In all United States casinos, employees on the game are called *dealers*, not croupiers, as is common for some types of dealers in Europe.

Dealers are generally responsible for three things:

- dealing the game in accordance with the casino's policies and procedures;
- handling currency and chip transactions at the table;
- treating the players in the manner prescribed by casino policy.

Period.

They aren't cardsharps trained to beat you, even though sometimes it might seem that way. In most cases, the dealer would be delighted to see you win. Winners are usually happier and a happy game is more fun to work. Winners normally are better tippers, too, and a large portion of the dealer's income comes from tips (known as "tokes" in the casino).

So, if you get on a losing streak, don't blame the dealer. Give yourself a break and try a different table.

Other Casino Employees

Aside from those employees and "bosses" who run the table games, there are others working in the casino you should become familiar with.

Casino Hosts

Casino hosts, as their name implies, are individuals who ease the workload of the pit bosses by taking care of the personal needs of casino customers.

Hosts normally have the "power of the pen"—they can approve complimentaries when appropriate. They often are called in advance by players to assist in making room or transportation arrangements, and, generally, they're available to help with anything and everything involving the customer's relationship with the casino.

Just as you would be a host to a guest in your home, casino hosts fulfill that function for guests of the casino.

In addition, most hosts have casino marketing responsibilities. For this reason, they're often found roaming around the casino introducing themselves to new or unknown players so they can add another name to their "book." The host's book often is the starting place for possible comps, invitations, and other preferential treatment that casinos offer their valued customers as inducements to come back often.

In most casinos, hosts come in two flavors—games hosts and slot hosts—to allow to them to specialize and focus their attention on one or the other.

Casino Credit Executives

Casino credit executives are to a casino what loan officers are to a bank. Players who wish to establish a line of credit with the casino make the arrangements with a credit executive, usually found in the casino credit office adjacent to the casino floor.

Casino credit executives and their bosses have varying authority to grant credit, just as bank loan officers do. Most credit executives can approve moderate credit lines, but larger lines normally require the approval of several levels of senior management. Each casino has a different philosophy on how liberal or conservative it wants to be with casino credit.

In Nevada, where the laws and regulations governing issuance of casino credit are less detailed, casino hosts are often credit executives as well. In Atlantic City, the two positions are separate.

Slot Department Bosses and Employees

Just as the table games have shift bosses, pit bosses, and floor persons, the slot department has shift managers, slot supervisors, and slot attendants.

Collectively, their job is to make sure the slot equipment is in proper working order, that hand-paid jackpots are delivered promptly, that slot machine coin hoppers are filled when necessary, and, most important, that the players are treated well.

If your slot machine jams, the first person you're likely to see is a *slot attendant*, who usually will be able to solve minor problems and answer any questions you may have. If the problem is more serious, a *slot technician* (formerly known as a slot mechanic before electronic slots became common), will come. In most cases, the slot technician will quickly be able to fix all but the most serious malfunctions.

By the way, today's electronic slot machines are controlled by an internal computer chip. *The chip controls the game* and, totally at random, generates jackpots and payouts. There's nothing the slot attendant or slot technician can do when they're tinkering around in there to make the machine start or stop paying. Honest, they simply don't work that way.

3

Casino Myths, Legends, and Superstitions

The very nature of casino gambling lends itself to a host of myths, legends, and superstitions. You might be surprised at what some people believe.

Cheating the Players

For example, do you ever wonder if you have been cheated by the casino? Not that it couldn't be done without you knowing it, but the chances of being cheated by a major casino in Nevada or Atlantic City are nil!

Why?

Think about it.

Casinos cost hundreds of millions of dollars to build. They generate millions of dollars in profits for the owners and stockholders. In short, they are big, big businesses. If any casino was caught attempting to cheat a player, the state regulators would shut the doors in a New York minute, and the managers could easily go to jail for a long time. No casino management would risk that to cheat any player—even for a substantial sum. It just isn't worth it, and it isn't necessary.

It isn't necessary because the advantage of all casino games favors the house. The longer you play, and the more people like you there are in the casino, the more the casino will win. (Not everybody loses, of course. If there weren't a lot of winners, no one would gamble.)

Believe it or not, the casino is only occasionally concerned about how much any individual player is winning or losing. In the long run, it doesn't make too much difference to us. We tend to look more at the big picture. As long as the casino is assured overall of coming out ahead week in and week out, we wouldn't risk it all by trying to cheat you out of a few bucks; we'll probably win it from you in the long run anyway. We know that; you should, too.

Having said all that, I will tell you flatly that all of those common myths you've heard aren't true.

- There isn't a button "upstairs" we can push to make the slot machines pay off.
- There isn't any switch on the Big Six Wheel or the roulette tables to control the number.
- We don't have "special" cards we bring out when somebody is winning big.
- We don't give the dealers cardsharp training to deal from the bottom of the deck.
- We don't pump pure oxygen into the air conditioning.
- We don't put little drops in the free drinks to make you lose control—you probably don't need our help for that, anyway.
- We don't cheat or welsh in any way, shape, or form.

36

Organized Crime

I sincerely hope that this doesn't come as a big surprise, but the casinos in Nevada and Atlantic City aren't run by mobsters.

It is documented fact that organized crime did control and skim a number of casinos in Las Vegas in the early days. In fact, one of the first major Las Vegas Strip casinos (the Flamingo, now owned by Hilton Hotel Corporation) was conceived and built shortly after World War II by Benjamin Siegel, also known as "Bugsy." Bugsy apparently had a business disagreement with his associates a short time later and his casino career was cut short— along with his life.

In the 1960s, major corporations began to build and acquire major casino hotels in Nevada. This trend, coupled with determined efforts by state and federal law enforcement agencies, eventually put the mob out of the casino business.

Today, all casinos in the United States are strictly regulated by the government and managers are subject to exhaustive investigations before being licensed to work in a casino. So, that pit boss you've been wondering about might be a member of the VFW or the PTA, but not the Mafia. Sorry. I hope I didn't burst your bubble.

Superstitions

Maybe because gambling is concerned with good luck and bad luck, most gamblers are superstitious by nature.

Players sometimes feel "luckier" in a certain casino...or at a certain slot machine...or with a particular dealer. Some players only come on certain days of the week. Others wear the same jacket or hat for luck.

Most hotels—and all casino-hotels—don't have a thirteenth

floor. Why? Simple. Nobody wants to stay on the thirteenth floor. Next time you're at your favorite casino, take a look at the floor numbers in the elevator...I'll bet you won't find thirteen.

Casino bosses tend to be just as superstitious as the players, although most of us won't admit it.

It's not uncommon to find a salt shaker hidden away in the pit somewhere. If one of the tables is losing bad, a little salt on the floor can't hurt, right?

I know a former Las Vegas pit boss now working in Atlantic City who believes a table's luck can be changed by scattering Keno tickets on the floor around the table. (Keno isn't permitted in Atlantic City, so this guy has the tickets sent to him periodically from Las Vegas.)

The Strangest Superstition of All

The strangest superstition I've come across originated with a shift boss at the casino where I work in Atlantic City.

We once went through a several-month period when the casino was just plain unlucky. We weren't winning enough at the tables. One day this shift boss—I'll call him Don—came on duty smiling.

"Hey, Boss," he said. "Our luck's going to change starting next shift."

"What makes you think so?" I asked.

"See this," he replied, pointing to a greenish-white blob on his shoulder. "A sea gull s--t on me when I was coming to work. That's good luck, didn't you know?"

Our luck changed that very evening.

Did the sea gull have anything to do with it?

I don't know, but every time our luck turns bad, the casino manager usually sends Don out to walk on the Boardwalk until he gets hit with some good luck.

4

Casino Security and Surveillance

Big Brother is watching

Casino executives are not only superstitious, most are also downright suspicious...especially when it comes to the casino's money. Most casino executives, like bankers, believe that sooner or later someone will try to rip them off. They're right; sooner or later, someone will try it.

This is why the daily working environment of all casinos is based upon consistent procedures, a lot of management and supervision, and constant observation. Everybody watches everyone else.

The floor persons watch the dealers and players...the pit bosses watch the floor persons...the shift bosses watch the pit bosses…the casino manager watches the shift bosses…the executives upstairs watch the casino manager…surveillance and security watch everybody…and the state regulators and enforcement agents watch us all watch each other.

It's not exactly an atmosphere based on mutual trust and belief in the inherent goodness of your fellow man. It's not meant to be.

In all large casinos, at any given time, there are hundreds of customers and often millions of dollars in cash and chips in circulation. Casinos and state regulators go to great lengths to prevent thefts, injuries, or disruption.

Believe it or not, most state gaming regulators are just as concerned about protecting the casinos as they are about safeguarding the interests of the players. By making it extremely difficult to cheat or rob a casino, a safer, more relaxing environment results for customers and employees alike.

Casinos normally have two separate departments for security and surveillance.

The security department is responsible for the physical safety and security of the casino, its patrons and employees. Uniformed security officers and plainclothes officers are always present. In Nevada, these officers normally are armed; in Atlantic City, they are not.

In addition to normal security guards, most casinos have several officers trained as paramedics or emergency medical technicians, who can respond quickly in the event of an accident or sudden illness.

The vast majority of the time, the mere presence of a lot of uniformed security officers prevents unwanted or dangerous situations from happening. When they're visible, those so tempted are much less likely to try something foolish.

Surveillance operators, however, see all but are seldom seen themselves.

The surveillance department conducts most of its protective

work with closed-circuit television. In most casinos, every single table game can be monitored in extreme detail by *several* television cameras. Operators in the surveillance room routinely and randomly switch other cameras around from table to table as additional coverage.

In addition to the gaming tables, all slot machine areas, the casino cage, change booths, the count rooms, other sensitive areas, and most elevators are constantly monitored by cameras. Most of what the cameras see is recorded on videotape equipment mounted in wall-size racks.

In covering a game by camera, an experienced operator can read every exposed card, count all bets, and differentiate between denominations of chips. When employees or players occasionally make moves that aren't part of the established procedures, they are taped from various angles for immediate reexamination to see if there is cause for concern.

To supplement the surveillance cameras, most casinos also are constructed with a system of catwalks and two-way mirrors in the casino ceiling. This enables surveillance operators to observe the action being simultaneously recorded by the video cameras. The ceiling observation area is known in all casinos as the "Eye in the Sky."

Surveillance and security are successful in preventing most thefts and stopping most cheaters and, of course, are a great asset in apprehending, indicting, and convicting those foolish enough to try. Almost all are discovered and, all too often, those caught either work for the house or are in cahoots with someone on the inside. In both Nevada and New Jersey, such activities are illegal and are prosecuted.

The result of these extensive protective measures is to discourage all but the most foolhardy thieves or potential cheaters from disrupting an atmosphere designed for your safety and enjoyment. It may seem like "Big Brother," but, unless you're planning the big casino heist of the decade, be comfortable knowing that it's all done to give you a safe, honest, secure experience in the casino.

The First Eye in the Sky?

Before such modern inventions as TV cameras and two-way mirrors, owners and casino managers used their naked eyes with peep holes in walls and ceilings.

There's a legend about one of the early casino pioneers at Lake Tahoe—let's call him Harry—who owned a small gambling club which later became quite large and famous. It's still there today.

Harry didn't trust anybody and, among other things, he kept a cot in the attic over the bar. There was a peep hole in the attic floor where Harry kept watch to be sure the bartenders were ringing up all the drinks and putting the money in the cash register.

Late one evening, as Harry had his eye glued to the peep hole, he noticed a bartender pause before ringing up a drink.

The bartender looked around to see if anybody was watching him, shrugged his shoulders and dropped the half-dollar into his vest pocket. Almost immediately, however, he became undecided and went over to put the money in the register.

Before ringing up the drink, though, he had another change of heart. He looked at the coin, tossed it in the air and called out "heads."

The coin came up "tails," whereupon the bartender shrugged his shoulders a last time and put it in his pocket anyway.

Harry was enraged.

"Hey, you son of a bitch," he yelled down. "Put that in the register....I won it, fair and square."

5

Casino Table Games

They're easy; don't be intimidated

Even though many casinos win more money from the slot machines, table games are still the heart and soul of most gambling establishments. Slots can be a lot of fun, especially with the ever-increasing varieties of games, but they can't duplicate the excitement of personal interaction found on the traditional casino table games.

None of the table games is hard to learn. The stakes aren't prohibitive, and the house percentage is less on the tables than on most slots. Why, then, are so many people—including those who play the slots or bet on the lotteries—afraid to play Blackjack, Craps, Baccarat, Roulette or the other games?

In a word, intimidation...also known as fear! Fear of losing too much money; fear of making a mistake; fear of looking foolish or ignorant; even fear of being cheated.

None of these is a good reason to miss out on a fun, exciting way to pass some of your time in the casino.

There are only three things you really should know about a table game before you sit down to play:

1. The basic rules of the game—how do you win or lose?
2. Some form of basic playing strategy.
3. A betting/money management strategy.

Items 2 and 3, playing strategy and money management, are beyond the scope of this book. There are numerous books on gambling systems and betting strategies designed to help improve your chances of winning. Some of the best are written by my good friend, John Patrick. They aren't expensive and, if you are about to give the tables a try, spend a few evenings with one of these good books.

But systems or not, you still have to know Item 1, how to play the game. The rest of this chapter will outline the basic rules of the most popular casino games. However, different casinos and locations often have slight variations on these basic rules, so be sure to ask about them at whatever casino you next visit.

Blackjack

The most popular table game in the United States is Blackjack, also known as "BJ" or "twenty-one."

Blackjack is really a simple game. Basically, each player is trying to get a higher point total than the dealer without going over a total of 21. Numbered cards count face value, face cards count as 10, and Aces can be either 1 or 11 at your choice.

While some casinos still deal single or double decks by hand, most casinos deal four, six, or eight decks from a box on the table called a "shoe." Each player initially places a bet in the marked area of the table layout. The players and dealer are then dealt two cards each.

In Atlantic City, the players' cards are dealt face up and you aren't permitted to touch the cards. This is increasingly common in Nevada, too, but some places deal the players' cards face down. In these casinos, pick up your cards when they're dealt. The dealer always receives one card face down and one face up.

When you get your first two cards, if they are an ace and a 10 or face card, you have Blackjack. The dealer will pay you 3 to 2 as long as he doesn't have Blackjack too. If he does, its a push or tie—too bad.

After you have received your first two cards and if you don't have a Blackjack, you need to decide whether to hit (draw additional cards) or stand (not draw).

If you want to stand or stop drawing, make a "stop" signal to the dealer when it's your turn by making a slight pushing motion with your palm toward the dealer. If you want another card, make a "come on" motion with your hand. Make your hand motions clearly and low on the table right behind your bet. Never touch your cards and leave your bet alone until the hand is over.

If you're playing in a casino where you hold the cards in your hand, signal a hit or draw by making a "come on" scratching motion with your cards on the table; if you want to stand, slide the edge of your cards face down under your bet and leave them there.

Remember, if you draw cards until your total is twenty-two or more, you bust (lose), period. When you have a total of seventeen or more, it's always wiser to stand and let the dealer draw. In most casinos, the dealer has to stand on any total of seventeen and draw on any total of sixteen or less. However, in downtown Las Vegas and in Northern Nevada, some casinos require the dealer to draw to a "soft 17" (a 6 and an Ace), which slightly increases the house advantage.

If your first two cards total 9, 10, 11 (or any other number if the casino rules permit it), you may "double down" if you think your chances of winning are good. Simply place an amount equal to your original bet *next* to it in the betting area and, when it's your turn to draw, say "Double Down." You may double for less than your original bet too. Just place your chips next to your original bet and say, "Double for less."

When you double down, the dealer will give you one card only, usually face down (face up in Atlantic City). When the hand is over he or she will turn your card over and you'll learn the news. (Don't get impatient and peek at it before then—it's bad luck and the other players will think you're a schmuck.)

If your first two cards are a pair (two of a kind), you may split them. When it's your turn, place an amount exactly equal to your original bet next to it and say "Splitting." Each of the two cards becomes a new hand and you may draw one or more cards until you stop or bust. However, when you split Aces, you'll only receive one additional card on each Ace. Some casinos will also allow you to double down after you've split a pair, so check the local house rules to find out—just ask a dealer or floor person.

The only other bet available in Blackjack is "insurance." When the dealer's up card is an Ace, he or she will ask for insurance bets. Betting on insurance means you think the dealer has Blackjack. You bet up to one-half of your original bet. If the dealer doesn't have Blackjack, you lose your insurance bet. If the dealer does have Blackjack, you will be paid two to one for your insurance bet. Your winnings will offset the amount you lose on your original bet; that's why they call it insurance.

All other bets in Blackjack are "even money." Whatever you bet is the amount you'll be paid if you win.

That's it for Blackjack. If it sounds like something you'd enjoy, give it a try. After all, it's the most popular casino game in the country.

Baccarat

Baccarat is one of the simplest casino games, even though its frequent high betting action intimidates many people.

The object of the game is to get as close to nine as possible—and you can't go over, or "bust," as you can in Blackjack. Aces count one, all other cards count face value except 10s and face cards, which count zero. Whenever your point total goes over nine, subtract the first digit to get your total. For example a 5 and 4 equal a total 9 (naturally). An 8 and a 9 equal 7 (17 minus the first digit).

No matter how many players are at the table, only two hands are dealt. One hand is called "bankers"; the other is called "players." The house doesn't have a hand—you can think of bankers and players as heads or tails if you want.

The only decisions you have to make are how much to bet and whether to bet on bankers or players. You can also bet on tie. Banker or player bets pay even money; ties pay eight to one. If you bet on the bank and win, you will owe a commission of 5 percent of your winnings. Your commissions are marked in an area next to the chip bank on the table with numbered markers called lammers. At the end of each shoe, or when you leave the table, you'll be asked to pay the commissions you owe.

Other than whether to bet banker, player, or tie, you have no options or decisions in Baccarat. The rules of the game decide whether the bank or player hands are entitled to draw an extra card. The dealers know the rules and will announce them clearly. I won't spell them out here, but you can get a copy at any casino with a Baccarat game.

The cards are dealt out of a shoe that is passed around the table from player to player. Each time the player hand wins, the shoe passes to the next player. The player with the shoe is called the banker, but he or she is still permitted to bet on player if desired.

The dealer instructs the banker how and when to deal the cards, so you don't have to be James Bond to handle it. You can also "pass the shoe" (decline to deal) if you want, but it's fun so you should at least give it a try.

That's it for Baccarat, except for Mini Baccarat. In Mini Baccarat, the rules are the same, with two differences. First, there's only one dealer and he or she deals all the cards—the shoe isn't passed around the table. Second, the table is smaller, just like a Blackjack table. Other than these two minor differences, Mini Baccarat is identical to the big table Baccarat games. One final thought: Baccarat is a lot of fun and it has the lowest house advantage available in the casino. Don't let fear or intimidation keep you from giving it a try.

Roulette

Roulette is another game that's easy to understand and easy to learn. The object of the game is to bet on an outcome determined by a little white ball falling into one of thirty-eight slots on a spinning wheel.

Sound easy? It is.

An American Roulette wheel has thirty-six numbers plus "0" and "00." The numbers 1 through 36 alternate in red and black; "0" and "00" are in green. On the table layout you can play each of the individual numbers by placing your bet directly on the one you want. You can also bet groups of adjacent numbers: 2, 3, 4, 5, 6, 12, or 18. The odds or payoff of these bets get smaller as the number increases. Any casino will give you a guide to the payoffs and a chart of how to place your bet on the layout.

There are also "even money" bets at the Roulette table. These are "high or low," "odd or even," and "red or black." These are known as outside bets because the betting box on the layout is "outside" the numbers. For obvious reasons, the number area of the layout is known as the "inside." All bets in Roulette are for the next spin of the wheel only, so each spin of the ball by the dealer is a new game.

The only tricky thing to remember about Roulette is that different chips are used in this game. When you buy in, you'll exchange cash or regular casino chips for Roulette chips good only while you're playing at that table. When you leave the table, the dealer will convert the Roulette chips back to casino chips which you can cash at the casino cage.

The chips at Roulette are different colors. Each player has his or her own color so the dealers can tell which bets belong to which players. Makes sense, right? Your chips can be worth whatever you want. If you buy in for $20 and tell the dealer you want fifty-cent chips, you'll get forty chips in your own color to use on that game. When you're ready to leave, slide your remaining chips toward the dealer and ask to cash in. You'll get regular casino chips in return.

In Roulette, whatever table minimum is posted is the minimum bet you can make on the *outside* bets. In other words, on a $5 table, you must bet at least $5 if you bet on high or low, odd or even, red or black. Your bets can be less on the inside numbers, but the total of your bets must add up to at least the table minimum. If you're betting the numbers on a $5 table, and your chips are worth $1, you must bet at least five chips—but you can spread these chips all over the inside if you want to.

Craps

Craps in a casino is a little more complex than street craps. In typical street or G.I. crap games, the shooter rolls for a point and bets with others on whether he'll make it or not. Casino craps (or "bank craps") offers many more additional bets and the casino "banks" the action, not the shooter.

In truth, Craps is more difficult to learn than the other games, but you can pick it up from a book on the game.

The basic game centers around two dice thrown by a player who is the "shooter." The dice pass around the Craps table among the players just like the shoe at the Baccarat table.

The shooter's first throw is known as the "come out roll." On this roll, 7 or 11 (a natural) wins; 2, 3, or 12 (craps) loses. Any other number becomes the shooter's "point," and the same shooter keeps on until he wins by rolling the point again or until he loses by rolling a seven.

Basic bets at craps are the "pass line" to bet the shooter will roll a natural or make his point, and the "don't pass line" to bet the shooter will roll craps or seven out. Bets on the pass line and don't pass line are paid even money.

There are many other bets in the game of Craps. Some are for one entire point, others are for one roll only. Some pay even money, others are bigger gambles and get paid at higher odds. Although a complete explanation of the game is beyond the scope of this chapter, you can learn all the basic wagers from any casino's free gaming guide and from observing a game for a half-hour or so.

Craps is a fast, exciting game and it offers a very low house advantage. It's also not just a "man's game." Some of the best Craps players I've seen are women. So, if you like nonstop action and a variety of potential wagers in a single game, craps is for you. Look into it.

Other Table Games

A number of other table games—some new, some old as the hills—are offered at many casinos, especially in Nevada where the law permits casinos to offer more variety to their customers. These games include, among others, Pai Gow, Sic Bo, Pai Gow Poker, and Red Dog (Acey-Deucey). Most casinos also have a Big Six Wheel (Wheel of Fortune), which needs no explanation. Poker and Keno are also common in Nevada, but these aren't considered casino table games.

Get In on the Action

While I haven't given you detailed descriptions of every game, I hope it's been enough to convince you that casino table games are fun, easy to learn and play, and offer fairly low house advantages for the player. If you're one of those who has been afraid to step up and take a chance, why not get your feet wet on your next casino foray? But, before you do, read on about the etiquette of casino table play...if you really want to be treated like a high roller.

6

Casino Table Games Etiquette

One thing I've noticed during my years as a casino executive is that many people who know how to play the games are afraid to sit down because they're not knowledgeable about the mechanics of playing in a casino.

In other words, they're not scared of the game, but they don't know how to do the simple things—like buying in or tipping the dealer—and they don't want to look foolish by making a mistake. If you've hesitated to play for this reason, here are some simple guidelines. Follow them, and no one will ever know you haven't been playing for years.

Joining the Game

At Craps, it's easy. If there's room to stand around the table, belly up and wait for the next come-out roll. (You don't have to wait, but you'll probably want to get a feel for the game first.)

At the other games where chairs or stools are provided, walk up to any empty chair and sit down. In Blackjack, players often play more than one spot, so be sure the empty stool you're eyeing isn't in front of a spot being played by someone else. If you're not sure, simply ask the dealer if that spot is free.

Buying In

When you join a game, the first thing you need to do is exchange your cash money for gaming chips. Wait for a pause in the action—between rolls in Craps or after the dealer has paid off all bets from the last hand in Blackjack, Baccarat, and Roulette. Put your cash on the layout within the dealer's reach and say, "Chips, please." There's no need to tell the dealer how much you want. He or she will count out your money on the table, give you an equivalent amount of chips, and drop your cash into a slot which leads to a locked drop box under the table. When you've finished playing, take your chips to the casino cage (cashier) to exchange them back into currency.

There is one exception—Roulette. When you buy in at a Roulette game (as previously noted) you receive special chips *good only for your use at that particular game.* In Roulette, each player has different color chips so the dealer can tell which bets belong to which players. When you buy in at a Roulette game, place your money on the table near the dealer and tell him or her what denomination chips you want. If you want your chips to be worth a dollar each, simply say, "Dollar chips, please." Casinos have different rules about what denominations they will allow in their Roulette games, so be prepared for the dealer to tell you if you've asked for too high or too low a denomination.

When you leave the game, shove your Roulette chips toward the dealer and say, "Cash me out, please." The dealer will exchange your Roulette chips for regular casino chips which you can use at another game or redeem for cash at the casino cage.

Placing Your Bet

Once you've found a spot in a game and have bought in, you're ready to place your first bet. Here's how to do it:

Blackjack: Place your bet in the betting area in front of you— be sure to bet at least the table minimum but not more than the maximum. If your bet consists of chips of different denominations, put the highest denomination chips on the bottom and the lowest on top. Once you've placed your bet and the hand starts, don't touch your bet until the hand is finished and the dealer has paid or collected the bet. If you double down or split cards during the hand, don't touch your original bet; simply place your additional bet *next to* your original bet—not on top of it. If you don't have the correct amount in chips for your double or split bet, just place a higher amount in chips or cash next to your original bet and the dealer will automatically make change and return the excess amount to you.

Baccarat: Place your bet in one of the three betting areas in front of your seat—banker, player, or tie. When the hand is over, your bet will be paid or collected by the dealer, so don't touch it again until then.

Roulette: Place your own bets wherever you want them, being certain the total of your "inside" bets and each of your "outside" bets is at least the table minimum. You can move, increase, decrease, or remove any bet up to the time when the dealer says, "No more bets, please." After that, wait until your bets are paid or collected before touching them again. By the way, in Roulette, when a bet is paid, the dealer will leave your original winning bet alone. Unless you want to make the same bet again on the next spin, be sure to take it down or move it.

Craps: Some bets you can place yourself—the easy-to-reach ones like pass and don't pass, come and don't come, field, etc. For bets in the center of the table or to place or buy a number, simply toss your bet onto the table and call out your bet. "$5 hard eight," or "$2 any Craps," for example. One of the dealers will acknowledge your bet, move your chips to the correct spot, and give you any change you may have coming. (Don't worry, they know by where they place the bet whom it belongs to...but don't change positions around the table too much.) There are many different wagers in the game of Craps. If you're not sure how to make a certain bet, just ask the dealer—it happens all the time and is no cause for embarrassment. After all, it's your money.

Minding Your Own Business

Some people tend to get vocally upset and angry when another player at the table does something they don't like. These people can get downright rude if you hit when they think you should stand, etc. If you're guilty of this type of behavior, and if nobody has mentioned before that it's out of line, it is.

One basic rule in any casino is since you're betting with your money, you get to bet however you want. If someone is doing things at your table that you just can't stand, there are two appropriate things you should do: 1. Keep your mouth and temper under control; 2. Find another table.

The same holds true with the dealer. If you're getting killed at the table, it isn't the dealer's fault. He or she didn't do it on purpose. Don't get mad, find another game and try your luck there.

What If the Dealer Makes a Mistake?

What should you do if you think—or know—the dealer has made a mistake? First, understand that it was most likely just that, a mistake. People make them all the time, even people who are casino dealers.

If you think the dealer hasn't paid your bet correctly, immediately call it to his or her attention in a quiet, polite manner. In most cases, the mistake will be corrected immediately. If it isn't and you're sure you're right, ask for the floor person. In most cases, disputes are resolved in the customer's favor, unless the customer is clearly wrong or asking for something that's out of line. In any event, you can be certain that 99.9 percent of all casino mistakes are unintentional and will be resolved cordially and quickly...we try to treat your mistakes the same way, too.

Tipping the Dealer

Common courtesy in a casino includes tipping the dealers once in a while, especially if you're winning. To tip a dealer, simply slide a chip in his or her direction and say, "For the dealer."

Another way to tip the dealer is to place a bet for him. Once you've made your own bet in Blackjack or Baccarat, place your tip to the side and slightly ahead of your bet. The dealer will know it's a toke (tip). If you win, the dealer wins too and keeps your tip plus the winnings. In Roulette or Craps, your tip can be any bet you want without regard to table minimum. Just make the bet and say, "This is for the dealer."

7

Slot and Video Gaming Machines

In your education on how to get treated like a high roller in a casino, don't make the mistake of thinking you have to be a table games player to get a comp. You can do it on the slots just as easily.

Most American casinos today win more from their slots than they do from the table games. Many of a casino's best customers are slot or video poker players and, believe me, these people get treated just as well as many high-roller Baccarat players.

The odds on slot machines vary. In Atlantic City, the state requires that machines hold no more than 17 percent—that is, they have to have an average return of at least 83 percent to the player. In most casinos, however, the machines are much more liberal than that, averaging between 10 and 13 percent.

On the other hand, New Jersey law prohibits casinos from advertising the odds on any casino game or slot machine, so don't expect to see the percentages advertised as they are in Las Vegas. Even when high payouts are advertised by Nevada casinos, don't assume that every machine will pay at those odds—after all, when chicken is on sale at the supermarket, you don't expect to get lamb chops at the same price, right?

One thing to bear in mind about slots is that higher denominations generally have better odds than lower ones. In other words, the odds are usually better on a dollar machine than on a nickel machine.

Slots—the traditional reel machines as well as the newer video poker ones—can be exciting. Also, they're a "private game" you can play by yourself at whatever pace is comfortable.

Let's talk about traditional reel slots. As you probably know, they've been around for a long time. In the beginning and until about thirty years ago, most slot machines were pure mechanical coin devices. By inserting a coin, the mechanism was released for the handle pull. The reels spun into action and stopped in random fashion generating various payouts.

These machines—the old one-armed bandits—were eventually replaced with electro-mechanical machines. These were simply electric versions of the old mechanical slots with a few new whistles and bells added. They were still basically machines with a lot of moving parts that would eventually get jammed or wear out.

Today's slot machines are all electronic machines. Basically, each machine is a little computer programmed to be a specific kind of game. They are more reliable than the older mechanical machines, they provide an endless number of variations of the games, and they're much more difficult to cheat or tamper with.

Most machines today—slots and video pokers—are multiple-coin machines controlled by a special computer chip. Just as a computer can be programmed to generate numbers totally at random, these chips are programmed to play a specific game, with each spin totally at random. Both the chip and the machine are inspected and tested by state gaming regulators before being allowed on the casino floor.

Payoffs on reel type slot machines are determined by three factors.

First is the game itself. The payoff table on the front of every machine will explain which reel combinations pay on that particular machine. They aren't all alike, so don't assume you'll get paid with two cherries or three bells—check first to see what combinations pay on the machine you've chosen. Some machines are designed to pay a frequent number of small wins—bell/fruit machines, for example. Others are "jackpot only" machines that pay out larger jackpots, but less frequently—single/double/triple bar machines, to name just one type.

The second payoff factor is how many coins you've played on that particular spin. This is something you should keep in mind. Most machines give you better payoffs—and better odds—when you've played the maximum coins. You should always do this. You never know when a large jackpot is going to hit. If you miss a big payoff because you only played one coin, shame on you! Doing this just increases the house's advantage over you. If you want to only play about one dollar per spin, don't play a dollar machine one coin at a time. Find a five-coin quarter machine and play five quarters every time you pull the handle.

The third factor on slot payoffs is the payout schedule. Even though one machine may pay on the same reel combinations as another, the amount paid can differ significantly. The super jackpot on one machine could be a few hundred dollars, while hitting the big one on another machine of the same denomination can be a life-changing fortune of several million. Take a close look at what the pay schedule is before you start to play. Just like people, slot machines are not all the same.

Many casinos in Nevada and Atlantic City have "linked progressive jackpot" machines. These machines are linked to other machines in the casino—or in many other casinos. Because the progressive jackpot builds with every play, the large number of machines can cause the jackpot to become enormous. If you play the slots because, as in the lottery, you want to take a shot at the big time, these are the machines to look for. Ask any slot attendant where the linked progressive machines are and knock yourself out.

One of the most popular introductions to casino gaming in recent years has been the video poker machines. These machines generally simulate a hand of five-card draw poker. They are multiple coin machines which display five cards when the "deal" button is pushed. You may keep or discard any or all of these cards and the resulting hand determines whether you win or lose. As in reel slots, always play the maximum coins or you risk losing big if you hit the Royal Flush.

The poker machines are simply a lot of fun. Many avid table game players also like the poker machines just as many slot players do. But, as with reel slots, poker machines are not all the same.

Most poker machines are "Jacks or better" machines. That is, if your final hand has a pair of jacks or higher, you'll win something. How much you win on each winning hand isn't always the same from machine to machine, so do some comparison shopping before you settle down to play.

There are a number of variations of video poker and new ones are being introduced all the time. Some popular ones include 10s or Better, Wild Card, Deuces Wild, Second Chance, and others. Video poker is the single fastest growing segment of casino gaming. If you haven't tried it yet, you may want to check these machines out on your next casino visit. They're fun.

The Big Jackpot Button in the Sky

I've mentioned several times already that the slot machines in today's casinos are controlled by a computer chip inside each machine. This means that there isn't some special switch we can throw to cause a machine to pay or not pay.

But some people just won't believe it.

We had a customer who came frequently and played the same dollar machine every time. He always played maximum coin and was playing for a huge jackpot worth over a million dollars. While he played a lot, the odds of winning a million dollar jackpot on a three dollar bet are pretty high—just like the lottery—and he hadn't hit it after about four months of frequent play.

Many of us at the casino got to know him and kept telling him he was trying for a real long shot. After a while, he came to believe that he'd played so much that he deserved to win. Most of us agreed with him, but there wasn't anything we could do about it.

"Push the button," he cried to one of our vice presidents one day.

"What button?" the perplexed VP answered.

"The jackpot button upstairs," he yelled, "I know you've got a button to make this machine pay off."

No matter how hard we tried to convince him to the contrary, he insisted that we had a jackpot button controlled by "the man upstairs."

Eventually, he started going to another casino and came in gloating one day after winning a nice jackpot.

"See," he said. "I got to know 'em over at _____, and they took care of me. Somebody upstairs was watching and pushed the jackpot button for me. Honest!"

8

Player Ratings

Fleas, whales, and other casino life forms

If you want to get treated like a high roller—or even a medium roller—by your favorite casino, you'll first need to understand how the casino determines where you fit into its spectrum of thousands of players.

High rollers are commonly referred to as "whales" by casino people—low rollers are sometimes known as "fleas." Identifying the whales and fleas and those in between is an important part of daily operations in the casino.

Why?

Obviously, not everybody can get a comp for dinner or a free room or a show on the house. So how do the casino executives and hosts determine who gets treated special and who doesn't?

Basically, we have to know at least two things about you before we can decide what kind of a roller you are. First, we need to know who you are. Sounds reasonable, right? But you'd be astounded to learn how many strangers come up in a casino and ask for a comp because they've "been playing a lot." Lesson one: To be treated like a high roller, the casino has to know who you are.

Next, after we know your name and where you're from etc., we need to know how your casino play compares with other players'. In other words, we want to know how much your casino play is worth to us. We look for answers to questions like: How often do you come? How long do you play? How much do you bet? What games do you play? Lesson two: To be treated like a high roller, the casino needs to know what you do when you're gambling.

In order for casinos to get to know their players by name and to find out about their level and style of casino play, we all have some form of player rating system for both games and slots.

When your play is rated in a casino, it means that someone is keeping track of how long you play, how much you bet and other information that will help us identify you as someone we might want to invite back or to whom we may wish to offer complimentaries and courtesies of the house.

While every casino has its own rating system, and even though these systems vary, they're basically all the same, so let me describe for you a generic casino rating system that's pretty close to average.

Give the floor person or pit boss your name when you begin to play at a table and ask to be rated. (I'll tell you about slot ratings in a minute). If you buy in for more than a few hundred dollars, or if you are a regular, you'll probably be rated automatically without having to ask, but be sure anyway—no rating, no comps.

Every game in the casino has a specific house advantage. Craps and Baccarat are about 1.5 percent, Blackjack is anywhere from 0 percent to 2 percent, depending upon the skill of the player, and

Roulette is about 4.5 percent. Also, every game in the casino has a certain "speed" or average number of decisions per hour.

Casino rating systems are usually mathematical formulas used to determine your *theoretical loss* while playing. Because all casino games favor the house, you will lose every time you play— *theoretically*. Everyone knows that some players win and some lose. Rating formulas are not designed to keep track of your actual wins and losses but rather to assign a standard theoretical value to your play so that it can be compared with the action of other players.

The basic formula used is normally something like this:

$$(\text{Average Bet}) \times (\text{Hours Played}) \times (\text{Game Speed}) \times (\text{Game Advantage}) = \text{Theoretical Loss}$$

If you play craps for four hours and your average bet is $10, your rating for that playing session would be:

$$\$10 \times 4 \text{ hours} \times 75 \text{ decisions/hour} \times .015 = 45 \text{ "points"}$$

This means that, theoretically, you lost $45.

Again, remember that we aren't talking about actual wins or losses. We assume that you'll win sometimes and lose at other times. We don't make comp decisions specifically on how much you lost—winners also get comped. So we use this theoretical formula to give us an average measurement that can be applied to all players the same way for fairness and objectivity.

Most casino rating formulas are more sophisticated and include factors for type, style, and skill of play. For example, a good card counter at Blackjack, if we discover he or she is a counter, will have a factor that reduces the theoretical loss to "0" because a card counter reduces the house advantage to zero.

Having said all this about rating systems—and almost all

casinos base most of their decisions on these systems—we also make an attempt to keep track of actual wins and losses. In big casinos, where players are more apt to move from table to table, this is often difficult and not very accurate, but we try anyway. We know that you won or lost real dollars, not theoretical ones.

Slot machine ratings are simpler. Most are done automatically by using a slot rating card that looks like any credit card. The card is inserted in a slot in a box attached to the machine. Just like an automatic teller machine, the customer's name is read from the magnetic stripe on the card and the system keeps track of the customer's slot action. Ask your favorite casino if they have slot rating cards and get one if they do.

The slot rating formula is simple, and is usually the amount of coin played multiplied by the house advantage of that particular machine. If your casino does not have a computerized slot rating system, ask to have your play manually rated by a slot host or slot attendant.

All of this stuff about player rating systems is pretty dull, I'll admit it. But if you want the casino to treat you like a high roller, you really need to know how we make those kinds of decisions. Just as a grocer can't afford to give everything away, neither can we. Ratings help us decide who gets "comped," how much, how often.

Most players would see their rating and say, "Wait a minute. I lost more than that. You guys don't know what you're doing!"

Right. We know that and we try to equate points with actual dollars. We use customers' average points per visit to decide who gets comp meals and rooms, who gets invited for special events and parties, who gets limos and air fares "comped" and so on. In making these decisions, we use the points for comparative purposes only and not as a hard dollar value.

The key here is to understand that casinos have specific systems and rules that determine what employees are and are not allowed to give away. Rating systems play a critical role in decisions that affect the way you'll be treated, so it will help you to understand a little bit about them.

More important, even if you don't really understand player rating, you should be aware that having your play rated is the first step on the way to being treated like a high roller. While your rated play may not qualify you for a comp, it's absolute fact that nonrated play, no matter how substantial, won't qualify you for anything at all.

The rule of thumb is this: If you want the casino to treat you right, be sure they know you and rate your casino action every time you play.

Now that the boring stuff is over, in the next chapter or two, I'll explain how these ratings can turn into free meals, rooms, shows, and all the other goodies casinos love to give away.

9

Casino Comps

To know you is to love you...sometimes

On some days, it seems like everybody in the casino wants a comp.

I've watched players sit down at a table, play $5 a hand for ten minutes, ask the pit boss for a comp dinner, and get irate when it is refused.

"Come on," these people will say, "it doesn't really cost you anything."

This is a common misconception. Many people actually believe that comps really don't cost the casino much. Comps do cost the casino. Food costs money. Labor costs money. Displacing a customer who might have paid cash costs money.

In other words, comps aren't free. They have value. Comps are intended as valuable courtesies extended by the house as a means of showing appreciation to good customers—those who risk sufficient amounts in the casino.

In the old days, no player would think of asking for a comp—it just wasn't done. Everyone understood that a complimentary meal or room would be offered by the house if the player's action warranted it. But, as casinos became larger and competition increased, comps were no longer a courtesy but a competitive tool used by various casinos to attract new players.

When Atlantic City opened for casino gaming in 1978, the casinos even began offering "comps" as incentives for people to take bus tours. A free lunch and a roll of quarters doesn't sound like much, but I know of casinos in Atlantic City that have given away more than $30 million a year in free rolls of quarters. That ain't hay, friends!

Anyway, today comps are much more common than they once were. For this reason, more employees in the casino have the authority to issue comps than in the old days when the shift boss was the only guy with the "power of the pen." With so many players asking for comps and with large numbers of employees having the authority to issue comps, casinos have to have policies and rules to keep this expensive practice under control.

How do casinos decide whether or not you deserve a comp?

Sometimes the decision is really a no-brainer. For instance, if you lose $10,000 in an hour and ask for a comp room or dinner, we'd probably not think twice.

But what if you played for hours, risked a lot of your bankroll, and ended up a big winner?

Obviously, you gave us a fair shot at your bankroll. You also have a big chunk of our money which we'd like to win back, so, chances are, we'll encourage you to stay by offering a comp in this case, too.

The question is really how much you were willing to put at risk in the casino over a reasonable amount of time.

Most comp decisions aren't so clear cut, however. That's why nearly all large casinos use player rating systems as the basis for comp guidelines which help their employees make sound decisions. A good comp policy is one which encourages employees to offer or extend a comp when it is warranted while minimizing the issuance to players who don't deserve them.

Just as player rating formulas vary from one casino to another, so do comp guidelines. Comps are a marketing tool just like advertising, promotions, discounts, etc. Each casino determines how much of its marketing budget it can afford to spend in each of these areas.

In most casinos, the comp guideline is usually expressed as a percentage of theoretical win. If, say, a certain casino's comp guideline is 30 percent of theoretical win, and your rating was one hundred points for the day, you'd be eligible for a comp worth about $30. Please notice I used the word eligible—not entitled. Comps are courtesies extended by the house—they're not part of your birthright.

If you've been playing for awhile and are being rated, the best person to ask for a comp is the floor person supervising your table. While the floor person may not be able to issue the comp, he or she will call the pit boss or a casino host. If you get turned down, ask what your play needs to be to qualify.

Please remember that casino employees are held strictly accountable for the comps they write, just as employees of all businesses are held accountable for their expenses. Every day the "man upstairs" gets a report that lists all comps issued by every employee and to whom they were issued. If the employee issues a comp that wasn't deserved, he or she will hear about it. Unfortunately, it's more difficult for management to discover how many comps were refused that should have been issued.

Theoretical loss, or points, should not be the only criterion taken into consideration by the casino when making a comp decision. Some customers come frequently, for instance, and, although on each individual visit they may not gamble enough to warrant a comp, their continued patronage should get them one from time to time just because they're regular customers. Like-wise, some players who make large bets and lose big in a short time won't generate many "points," but they may still qualify for a comp because of the magnitude of their loss.

Issuing comps isn't an exact science—it requires a decision. The more you know about how that decision is made, the easier it will be for you to get a comp when your play warrants one.

Another thing to consider if you're looking for comps is to find the right casino. Remember that each casino has a policy for issuing comps to *its* better players. If you like to hang out in a casino that caters to Arab oil sheiks and members of the Young Millionaires Club, your play may not look very impressive. You'd do better playing at a casino that caters to more of a middle-of-the-road crowd where your action may be heavy enough to get recognized.

One other tip worth considering is to play at a table with a lower minimum than you intend to bet. If you're going to bet $25 to $50 per hand, for example, your chances of getting rated and "comped" are better if you play at a $5 table. The reason is simple. If you're the only one betting $50 at a table where everyone else is betting $5 or $10, the floor person and pit boss are more likely to notice you. This may influence their comp decision more than if you were just one of the crowd at a $25 table.

Bonus Points

One of the most difficult aspects of comps is that there is no easy way to make the decision. While some casinos have tried to computerize the process, no computer can make the sort of common-sense business decision required to be a good casino comp issuer.

One common mistake made by casino hosts is to base all of their decisions on theoretical win, or "points."

We once had a host, I'll call him Mike, who loved to write comps. He had a large following of players who knew how to take advantage of the system. They came frequently and would quickly leave when they were unlucky, rarely losing much. When they were winning, however, they would bet enormous sums and rack up a lot of "points" in the rating system.

Frankly, they were smart players—they play the way I play...but I don't expect to get comped; I expect to win and buy my own dinner with the casino's money. But, because they had a lot of points, Mike wrote a lot of comps. The more comps he wrote, the more often they came, the more often they came the more points they generated, etc.

Finally, one day I asked Mike about all the comps he'd written for players who consistently beat the hell out of us. "Well, boss," he said proudly, "look at the points these guys have in the casino."

"You're right, Mike," I responded. "How would you like it if I asked payroll to issue your next paycheck in points instead of dollars."

Mike's comping decisions improved immediately.

10

How To Get a Comp

And when to avoid one

Most people I meet in the casino think that high roller treatment is all about comps.

They're wrong.

Real high rollers don't even think about comps—they get them automatically without having to ask. Real high rollers are big bettors who often wager more on a single hand than the value of all their comps.

In other words, if you have to ask for a comp or if you wonder whether you qualify for one, you're not a high roller or anything close to one.

Now that I've got that off my chest, I'll say again that you don't have to be a high roller to get a comp. You can get all kinds of comps and partial comps and in this chapter I'll give you some tips on how to do it.

Nevertheless, you should know up front that people who gamble to get comps are suckers. Casino executives know exactly how much it costs to issue a comp. We also know that we need to win more than we spend. So that free dinner you get for a comp isn't free at all...it probably costs you three or four times more than if you simply ordered and paid cash.

The best way to get a comp is to learn how to play and manage your bankroll to increase your chances of winning. Then you can forget the comps and buy your own dinner with your winnings. The casino pays the bill just like a comp, but you can go home feeling like a winner, not a sucker who blew a small fortune just to get a free steak dinner in the casino restaurant.

"Yeah, right," you say, "just tell me how to get a comp to the deli."

Okay, no more lectures. Let's talk about comps. Here are some things you can do to increase your chances of getting a comp.

1. First of all, you know you must get rated—every time you play, every time you change tables or machines. Make sure the casino has a record of all your action, because this will determine the extent to which you are comped. Also, while you're playing, get to know the floor person at your table and make sure he or she will get to know you and remember you.

2. Find a casino you like and do most or all of your gambling there. If you spread your action around two or three different casinos, you may not qualify for a comp at any of them, whereas at one place your combined total action will more likely qualify.

3. Make an effort to get to know a casino host at your favorite casino. Look him up every visit and start calling him to help make your reservations and arrangements, even if they aren't comped. Many comp decisions are borderline calls which could go either way. If the person making the decision knows you and sees you in

the casino frequently, the decision is more likely to go in your favor.

4. If you and your spouse go to the casino together, make sure both of you get rated. Even though neither of you individually may qualify for a comp, your combined action may put you over the top. When asking for a comp, remind the host or pit boss to check the action for both of you.

5. If your favorite casino has a club, mailing list, or rating card program, be certain to participate—along with your spouse. Usually, card holders and club members are the first to receive special offers, discounts, and freebies from the casino. Why? Simply because they know who you are and how to reach you.

6. If you normally don't qualify for a comp room, ask for one at casino rate. Usually, this will work and you'll get at least a 50 percent discount. The difference you save could mean as much as a comp meal or show.

7. Visit the casino at off times—midweek rather than weekends. During peak periods, comps are harder to get unless you're a pretty heavy player. During slower times, when the demand on restaurants, guestrooms, and showrooms is lighter, you're more likely to get a comp that would be refused on a Saturday night.

8. Give the pit boss a choice other than yes or no. Instead of asking for dinner for two, yes or no, ask if your comp should be for you and your guest or just you. Most comps are issued for two and he might not think to do it for one only. This could give him an opportunity to say yes rather than no. And, let's face it, a comp for one is still a comp. It will save you half price on a meal for two.

9. Try asking for a room comp rather than dinner in the restaurant. The reason is that all room comps are charged at a fixed rate. Meal comps, depending on how much you eat and drink, can be unpredictably expensive, a fact that scares many casino employees when they issue a comp for dinner. If you can get your room comped, use the money you save to pay for dinner.

10. Make sure the casino feels it made the right decision by comping you. Don't abuse the comp and order more extravagantly just because it's free. Leave an adequate tip. Look up the "comper" later in the casino and say thank you (also let him see that you're back in action) so you'll be remembered next time.

11. If you ask for a comp and are refused, ask how much more action you need to qualify. Be polite and courteous because the pit boss or host is merely carrying out casino policy...it isn't personal.

12. If your favorite casino routinely turns you down, shop around for a casino that is a little more liberal with comps. Sooner or later, you'll find a place that's right for your style and level of play.

13. Finally, remember that, no matter where you play, you won't get something for nothing. Comps are for players, not freeloaders. If you really don't play enough to get a comp, don't expect one.

Earlier in this chapter, I mentioned that playing for comps is a sucker move.

It is.

Every time you get a comp, you will, on the average, risk losing three or four times as much in the casino. Sure, comps are a bargain, but you can go broke in the casino trying to get a free meal. If playing for a comp causes you to play longer or for higher stakes than you can afford, sooner or later your time in the casino will become a nightmare, not a fun way to escape and relax for a day or two.

There Ain't No Free Lunch

Sometimes, players determined to get a comp for dinner begin to see things way out of proportion.

Not long ago, there was a woman, Mrs. G., playing Blackjack in our casino. She had been playing well for several hours, her bets ranging from $5 to $15. At the end of about three hours, even though she wasn't a big bettor, she was winning about $80—not a fortune, but not bad.

She asked the pit boss for a comp for dinner for herself and a guest. After checking her action, the pit boss politely told her that she'd need to play for another hour or two to qualify.

At this point, Mrs. G. should have left the table and used some of her winnings to buy dinner. She could have eaten a free dinner and still gone home with more money than she came with.

No way.

She increased her bets to $25 and sat through a monumental losing streak for two more hours. When the smoke cleared, she had lost the $80 she won plus $400 of her own money.

In the end, she got a comp dinner for herself and a guest. The value of the comp was $58.

She went home happy. Can you believe it?

11

Clubs, Rating Cards, Group Comps, and Assorted Freebies

In a casino, the only way to really be treated like a high roller is to be...you guessed it...a high roller.

However, as you've already learned, there are all sorts of things you can do to get the casino to treat you like somebody who's more special than the rest of the crowd. Your knowledge of how casinos work and how decisions are made will certainly set you apart as a "player." This, in itself, goes a long way toward improving how you're treated and thought of by the casino bosses.

Moreover, by becoming better known in your casino and more knowledgeable about what goes on there, you're likely to learn more about special offers, discounts, clubs, and other "deals" that may not be generally known.

Here are some things you should check on at your favorite casino. If they aren't offered, shop around for another place.

Casino Clubs and Rating Cards

Because comps often tend to be based more on current play than on regular patronage over a long period of time, many of a casino's customers—those who are small bettors who come frequently—often get lost in the crowd. This is unfortunate, because good, steady "regular" customers are as important to a casino as they are to any other business.

For this reason, many casinos—both in Atlantic City and in Nevada—have developed special "players clubs" which give rewards, benefits, and comps to these customers.

More than anything else, the increasing use of computer systems in casino management has made the rapid expansion of these clubs possible. A typical casino club, whether for slots, tables, or both, is usually based on a rating card. It typically has a magnetic stripe on it like a credit card and is used to identify the player and automatically keep track of his or her casino action.

What happens next differs from casino to casino. In some places, the casino allows each player to build up a "bank account" of points that can be used like trading stamps for goods and services within the casino or hotel. For instance, you might play $40 dollars in a slot machine and find out that you have received credit for five points in your "account." When you accumulate enough points, you can trade them in for a comp.

Other clubs are more sophisticated. At my casino, for example, the club is used to generate several actions. First, based upon your level of play, the casino will mail you a "check" the very next day which can be redeemed for cash on your next visit—sort of a "head start comp." The amount of the "check," of course, is based on the amount of your casino play on the last visit.

In addition, the ratings generated by club members are used for a whole series of monthly and more frequent mailings. Each month, all members whose average play per visit meets certain criteria receive special offers on room discounts, show tickets, and meal deals. Whenever the casino plans a special event, tournament, or party for its customers, the club members, again, are the first to get notified with special rates and offers.

Other benefits often include free gifts, preferred seating in the restaurants and showrooms, drawings, etc.

Now I know that these things don't appeal to everybody and they aren't the same as getting a free trip to the gourmet room courtesy of the pit boss. On the other hand, you can play at whatever level is comfortable for you and still get rewarded without getting in over your head.

How can you find out which casino club is right for you?

Shop around.

Most casinos allow you to join the club just by asking. Become a member of several. Play in each casino in your normal way and see what happens. Sooner or later, one casino club will start to be more appealing to you. When this happens, switch all of your business to that casino and start collecting your benefits as a "preferred player." In many ways, it makes you feel just like a high roller and it isn't nearly as risky.

By the way, if you routinely gamble with your spouse, ask the casino if they can put your two memberships together. In this way, both of your casino ratings will count together and you may be eligible as a couple for benefits you wouldn't get individually.

As in any other consumer promotion, not all "special casino deals" are likely to be worthwhile for everyone.

Some casinos, including several in Las Vegas, routinely run advertisements where they promise thousands of dollars of "free" casino action, food discounts, gifts, etc.). While, technically, they deliver on their promise, there's a lot of fine print. The quality of what's received is often disappointing to those who paid for the "free" deals. As in everything else in life, if the deal seems too good to be true, it probably is.

Group Comps and Discounts

One aspect of discounts available at many casinos is often overlooked by customers—group comps and discounts.

The theory is simple. If you arrange for a group to come to a casino for a party or banquet, and if the group you bring gambles in the casino while they're there, you may be able to get a discount for your function.

Casinos routinely give discounts for charity banquets, weddings, Bar Mitzvahs, and other functions simply based upon the propensity of certain kinds of people to gamble. For example, most veteran casino executives can tell you from experience what types of groups are most likely to be gamblers.

Among ethnic groups, Italians, Jews, Chinese, and Greeks all tend to be very good casino customers. Labor groups usually are better gamblers than professional or corporate or trade groups. Independent business owners and entrepreneurs gamble more than corporate executives.

Suppose your charitable group or lodge is looking for a place to hold their annual banquet. After discussing the menu and price with the catering director at your favorite casino, go talk to the head of casino marketing and ask if they would discount part of the cost because of your group's propensity to gamble.

If you can provide the casino with a list of those who will attend and prove that many of them are frequent casino players, you may get a break. If not, and if the casino has a rating card or club, ask if all your guests can get a rating card upon arrival. Then ask if you could be eligible for a discount after the fact, based on your guests' actual casino action on the date of your function.

The casino may not go along with your request, but it can't hurt to ask. I've seen it done many, many times, so don't be afraid to give it a shot. Your guests will have a great time as well.

The Man Upstairs Will Take Care of It

Speaking of group discounts reminds me of an incident at another Atlantic City casino eight or nine years ago.

I was the new vice president of marketing and had recently started dating the hotel's catering director, Susan, who later became my wife. Late one Saturday evening, I was waiting to leave with Susan, but she was in deep conversation with a customer, whom we'll call Sam, who was planning a major banquet for a large Philadelphia charity.

Finally, I walked over and quietly joined them at the table in the ballroom where they were seated. Susan briefly introduced me by name and they went back to their discussion.

"This menu is elegant," Susan said, "but it's going to be pretty expensive. It's going to put you over your budget."

"Oh, don't worry," responded Sam. "These people are players. The man upstairs will take care of it."

I started to get interested in the conversation.

Susan said, "Well, these centerpieces are very costly. We could do something nice for you that won't cost you nearly as much."

"Small potatoes," said Sam. "They're not that extravagant. The man upstairs will take care of it, no sweat."

"I don't know," Susan replied. "I think you may be expecting too much. At any rate, the flaming Baked Alaska and the Dom Perignon have to go—they'll put you over budget by a fortune."

"Nonsense," Sam said tartly. "How many times do I have to tell you—the man upstairs will take care of it."

Finally, I felt compelled to say something.

"This looks pretty extravagant to me," I interjected quietly. "I don't think the casino will be able to pick up nearly this much of the cost."

"Yeah, yeah," said Sam. "The man upstairs will pick up the tab for this one, believe me."

"No, he won't," I replied.

"Of course he will," Sam exploded. "Who the hell are you anyway?"

"I'm the man upstairs," I said with a smile. "Let's discuss a deal that makes sense for both of us."

Sam's group had a great function and the casino did discount a reasonable portion of the cost. Moreover, Sam and his wife became good friends of ours and a few months later were guests at our wedding.

What a great business!

12

Casino Credit

"Marker, please."

One of the most commonly held misconceptions about casinos is that only real "whales," high, high rollers, have credit lines.

You can get a credit line at a casino for as little as $500 if you want to. You don't have to be Daddy Warbucks.

Why bother?

There are lots of reasons why players prefer to have a line of credit at the casino. One of the best is that they don't want to carry around more cash than they have to. Another reason is that it's easier to keep track of your wins and losses if you're a frequent player.

Some players like a credit line simply because it makes them feel good to walk up to a table and call for a marker.

Establishing a line of credit at a casino is no more difficult than applying for a credit card or buying a new refrigerator on time at Sears. Here's how it works.

To apply for a credit line, go to the credit department, usually located on or just off the casino floor, and ask to see a credit executive. You'll be asked to complete a credit application just as you would for any other consumer loan.

Before approving a credit line, the credit director will look at all the same things a loan officer at a bank would. Basically, lenders normally are interested in two things—your ability to repay the loan and your credit history which verifies prompt payment of other debts.

A casino is no different. We want to make sure that your income is sufficient to repay the loan and that you're the kind of person who has a good credit history. Beyond that, however, a casino credit director will also check out your gambling history. Just as all businesses have national credit bureaus to check your credit record (we use them, too), casinos have an organization to keep track of those individuals who have used credit at a casino.

The credit executive wants to know if you normally gamble an amount consistent with the credit line you are requesting.

Why?

Simple. Casinos don't charge interest. The money we lend is expected to be played in the casino and repaid promptly. We are in the gambling business, not the no-interest, free loan business. So even though you may be in a financial position to repay a large credit line, if you don't normally gamble that much, the casino is unlikely to loan it to you unless you do.

It's a good idea to apply for your credit line ahead of time. Because the credit department will perform normal bank and credit checks after receiving your application, it's often not possible to grant approval on the spot, especially at eleven o'clock on a Saturday night when your friendly local banker is at home in bed.

The best procedure is to stop in and get a credit application and take it home to complete. Drop it in the mail a week or so before your next visit. When you next get to the casino, your line, if approved, will be ready for you to use. All you'll need to do is verify your identity and sign one or two forms.

To make use of your new credit line, simply go to one of the gaming tables and ask for a marker. After a few minutes, the floor person will bring the marker for your signature and will instruct the dealer to give you the appropriate amount in chips.

A casino marker is like a counter check—it can be submitted to your bank for payment just as any other check. Normally, the casino waits for a specified period of time before putting through the marker for payment. This allows time for you to redeem it for cash or for a regular check. You should check with your particular casino to learn the specific local repayment requirements.

After playing on credit, when you go to the casino cage to redeem your chips for cash, you'll be asked to apply the chips toward your marker. If you've won, you get your winnings in cash; the remaining chips are used to redeem your marker. If you've lost, you'll probably be asked to apply your remaining chips toward the marker and then will be expected to repay the difference in accordance with casino policy and local gaming regulations.

Don't make the mistake of thinking that markers are only for table game players. Many slot and video poker players have credit lines and use them regularly. Ask your casino credit executive what the procedures for slot markers are in the casino where you play.

Many people fear casino credit because they believe we might send some goon out to collect the next day. Casino credit collection practices are the same as any other business. If you don't or can't pay, we'll contact you and attempt to work out a repayment schedule. If you refuse to honor your debt, it will, like most other bad debts, be turned over to a collection agency or, in New Jersey, an attorney. In Nevada and New Jersey, casino credit debts are legally collectable.

If for any reason you have a problem with repayment, the smartest move is to contact the credit department and work out a repayment program. Don't worry about somebody like Rocky Balboa knocking on your door with a baseball bat.

A Whale Tale

While casino credit lines can be as small as $500, some of them are huge.

In Las Vegas, I was a senior vice president at the most expensive high-roller casino in the world. We had a player—a Middle Eastern gentleman living in Europe—who gambled for millions of dollars whenever he visited the casino.

On one visit, we expected him to play with $600,000 he had left on deposit in the casino cage. Instead, he requested $2 million on his credit line and we gave it to him.

He began to play Baccarat for high stakes and, within an hour or two, he lost the entire $2 million. He paid his marker immediately with a wire transfer from a Swiss bank and asked for another $2 million marker. He lost that and paid it; then he lost another $2 million and paid that off.

Finally he got his $600,000 from the cage and lost it all except for $100,000—then his luck changed and he started to win.

By the time his play had finished he had won back his entire $6.6 million plus another $400,000, for a grand total of $7 million.

He asked the cage to pay him with two checks—one for $5 million and another for $2 million—and he left for home.

The $2 million check was cashed within a few weeks, but he didn't cash or deposit the $5 million check for over nine months. We later learned that he kept the check in his wallet. When *gambling with his friends in Europe, he would casually let the check drop out of his wallet and pass it around to show that he'd "beat" our famous casino for $5 million.*

It just goes to show that it takes all kinds, I guess. How much interest do you think he wasted by not depositing our check in his Swiss bank?

13

Sorry, no chapter 13.
See chapter 3,
"Superstitions"

14

Junkets

Free vacations...or are they?

What, exactly, is a junket?

Traditionally, a junket is a free trip to a casino—a trip that costs you nothing. Supposedly, the free trip is offered to you because you're a high roller in the casino.

This definition was true years ago, but not today.

These days, few casinos run these old-fashioned junket programs because most aren't profitable for the casino.

Lets face it. Would you really risk losing enough in the casino to pay for the cost of air fare, room, food, and beverage for you and your spouse? Not many people will—especially in the last few years when air fares have become a lot more expensive.

The old junket programs are history.

Even so, there are quite a few casino tour programs that are advertised by their organizers as "junkets." Usually, these programs require you to spend a minimum amount to cover air fare and room. Everything else is "free"—as long as you play a certain amount each day in the casino.

Is this a bad deal?

No, it's often a good deal—as long as your requirement to play doesn't exceed the amount you would normally risk in the casino. In such a case, the other goodies are a real bargain.

On the other hand, if the rules require you to gamble beyond your means, take a second look and be sure the "free deals" are really worth what you might lose.

One thing you might want to explore is the "non-junket junket." Many casinos in Nevada and Atlantic City have special packages which offer good rates for your room, certain free meals, drinks, and shows—all with no specific requirement to play in the casino. If you do play to a level where you qualify for a comp, so much the better. You should be able go find out about special packages just by calling the reservations or sales department of the casino you're interested in visiting.

Another relatively recent development is a nationwide independent club for casino players, *Players Club International*. For an annual membership fee, Players Club offers its members excellent deals at casinos and resorts all over the world.

Typically, hotel rooms are at half price, meals and shows are discounted 25 to 50 percent, and air fares are fairly inexpensive. Additionally, they publish a regular "hotsheet" with special deals and tournaments at their various member casinos. If you're a frequent visitor to casinos, a membership in this club will pay for itself in no time.

15

The Casino Explosion of
of the Nineties

Riverboats, Indian reservations, and
other new jurisdictions

When I began writing the first edition of this book in 1990, legal casino gaming was still, by and large, a unique pastime limited to traditional games and available in this country primarily in Nevada and Atlantic City. Have things changed since then? You bet!

Today, even though Nevada and New Jersey are still the "big enchiladas" of the casino gaming industry in the United States, other states have legalized various forms of casino gaming. Moreover, as a result of federal laws which permit gaming on some Native American reservation lands, casinos exist in many other places in the country as well.

Not surprisingly, with this rapid expansion into other jurisdictions, we have seen a renewed interest in traditional casino games as well as the introduction of several table games which are rapidly growing in popularity. With this in mind, many readers, as well as numerous customers at my casino in Atlantic City, have asked about these new places to play and about the new, unfamiliar games.

For this reason, as this second edition was being prepared for printing, the publishers asked if I would add some information about the changing face of casino gambling. What does it take to be treated like a high roller in Iowa or Missouri? How does one play games like Caribbean Stud Poker, Pai Gow Poker and Red Dog? Okay. With the understanding that things are changing so fast that there may be new jurisdictions and even newer games by the time this book hits the street, here's a wrap up of the casino world at the time of this writing in early 1996.

Native American Casino Gaming

Before getting into the various new legal casino states, let me mention a few things about Indian casinos. Under a federal law called the Indian Gaming Regulatory Act, certain types of gaming may be permitted on Native American reservation trust lands in the various states. There is a strict process the Native American tribe or nation must go through in order to have a casino on its reservation.

Under federal law, generally speaking, if a state allows any type of gambling, even charitable gaming like "Las Vegas nights" played with scrip or play money, an Indian nation with a reservation located within that state may apply to have a casino where the same games are permitted for profit. In other words, if your state, for example, allows churches and synagogues to run mock casino games to raise money, an Indian reservation in your state could be permitted to run the same games for profit.

The federal law is complex; each situation is unique, so please understand that my description of the process is a very general oversimplification. Nevertheless, the law does exist and there are dozens of Native American casinos in states throughout the country as a result. How are they? Just like most other casinos (and most other businesses), some are great; others aren't so hot. Bear in mind that an approved Native American casino establishes its own rules and regulations, based upon agreement with the state and federal government. Many Indian casinos adopt casino procedures and regulations like those that are used in Nevada or Atlantic City, but they don't have to. So, don't be surprised if the procedures, rules, and regulations aren't the same as those you may be used to somewhere else.

Indian casinos run the gamut from small, poorly-run establishments to large, glamorous operations equal to anything available in Atlantic City or Las Vegas. One of the largest casinos in the United States (in terms of annual casino revenues) is the huge Foxwoods Casino in Ledyard, Connecticut. Owned by the Mashantucket Pequot Tribe, it has been fantastically successful and is well worth a visit if you live in or are visiting New England. You'll find the casino procedures and rules at Foxwoods similar to those in Atlantic City, upon which its policies were modeled.

Dozens of other states have Native American casinos. I've visited some very nice ones in Minnesota, Wisconsin, Washington State, New York, and California to name a few. If any of these casinos are near you, why not stop in for a visit? You might be pleasantly surprised. If not, don't go back.

In terms of being treated like a high roller, don't expect to be comped as readily or as generously at an Indian casino as in Atlantic City or Nevada. Most Indian casinos are located in out-of-the-way areas and many are "the only game in town." For this reason, they don't really need to comp their customers much, because they'll probably get the business anyway. In general, with Native American casinos, the bigger and fancier it is, and the closer it is to competing casinos, the more generous its comping policies are likely to be.

One other aspect of Native American casinos worth keeping in mind is the fact that Indian casinos are located on sovereign land and are not subject to the laws and courts of the state. This means that if you have a complaint about something, the authority you address your complaint to is likely to be a tribal gaming commission, not a representative of the state unless the Indian tribe negotiated such an arrangement with the state government.

So, even if your state doesn't have legalized casinos, it's entirely possible that one or more Indian casinos may be near to you and would be worth a visit. Many Native American tribes and nations suffer from extreme poverty and their people benefit greatly from the revenues generated by their casinos, even the smaller ones. So, don't hesitate to give them some play if you live or travel near one of them.

Colorado

Colorado is one of only four states that allow land-based casino gaming—in addition to New Jersey and Nevada, the other state is South Dakota.

In Colorado, casinos are limited to three small towns—Central City, Black Hawk, and Cripple Creek, which, together, have about sixty or seventy casinos. In general, the casinos are small when compared with Las Vegas or Atlantic City, but these three old mining towns are part of Colorado's colorful frontier history and the casinos offer limited, but entertaining gaming.

In Colorado, you'll find state-of-the-art slot and video gaming machines as well as live poker and blackjack. A maximum bet limit of $5 applies to all games, and no gaming may take place between 2:00 AM and 8:00 AM. I understand that parking is still somewhat of a problem, as are hotel and motel rooms for overnight visitors, but new construction should address these irritations in short order. Because Colorado's casinos are small, don't expect generous comps. Nevertheless, there are a lot of casinos and they are very competitive, so don't hesitate to ask.

Illinois

Illinois allows legal casinos on riverboats. Unlike some other states, there are no state-mandated limits on maximum wagers or on the amount you may risk during your visit. However, the Illinois boats are required to cruise. If navigational or mechanical problems prevent a boat from cruising, the casino is required to simulate cruising by limiting access to and from the boats for specific periods of time.

The Illinois riverboat casinos are excellent in every respect. Most are run by large, experienced casino companies and the gaming rules are similar to those you'll find in New Jersey and Nevada. Currently there are about a dozen boats located throughout the state. If you live in, or travel to, Illinois, I think you'd find a cruise on one of their boats worthwhile.

Indiana

As in Illinois, gaming in the Hoosier State is limited to cruising riverboat casinos on certain rivers if approved by the local county. As of this writing, one boat is now operating in Evansville in the southern part of the state, while others are in construction with openings planned throughout 1996. Both slots and table games are allowed and, like Illinois, the boats must actively cruise for gaming to take place.

Iowa

Iowa was the first state to allow riverboat casinos. Initially, the state placed certain limits on amounts which could be wagered as well as per-trip limits on the amount of money an individual could lose in total. As other states began to legalize riverboat casinos with no such limits, Iowa's casino industry began to suffer from a loss of business and, as a result, these limits were eventually rescinded.

Iowa's riverboats are located in some grand old river towns like Davenport, Bettendorf, and Council Bluffs. All types of games and slots are available and the casinos I've visited were very competitive in offering package deals to attract customers. While this isn't exactly like a traditional comp, finding the right deal can make your day more fun and less expensive. Another nice feature about Iowa's riverboat casinos is that the law only requires them to cruise a certain number of days each year. At other times, customers have free access at any time to use the casino which is in full operation at the dock.

Louisiana

The State of Louisiana, which always has been somewhat unique in many ways, is just as unique in its legalization of casino gaming. Most legal gaming in Louisiana is done on cruising riverboats with rules similar to other riverboat states. The boats are required to cruise, but gaming is allowed dockside if the boat is unable to cruise for acceptable safety or navigational reasons. There are no betting or loss limits.

In addition to its riverboat casinos, though, Louisiana authorized one large land-based casino for the city of New Orleans. This one casino has had its share of trouble. It began operating at a temporary site but was forced to close because of cost overruns.

It subsequently reopened on a smaller scale, but at the time of this writing there remains some doubt as to whether or not the ultimate permanent casino will ever open. Louisiana has long been known for the uniquely passionate flavor of its political processes, and the political atmosphere which surrounds Louisiana's casinos is no different.

The casinos themselves, however, are handsome, well-run operations and are definitely worth a visit if you live nearby or visit the state. All traditional casino games, slots, and video poker are available and the gaming rules will be familiar to you. Also, Louisiana allows limited video poker gaming at certain truck stops throughout the state.

All in all, the rules tend to change more frequently in Louisiana, so if you're not sure about something in a casino there, it would be best to ask a casino supervisor for the current information.

Mississippi

Mississippi is unique in its approach to casino gaming. There is no legal land-based gaming, nor is there any gaming on cruising riverboats. In Mississippi, all gaming is done in dockside facilities. The casinos themselves are elaborate structures built on floating barges which are permanently moored to the dock. This makes for some very unique casinos indeed. They are bigger and more elaborately designed than a traditional riverboat, yet they also are constrained by the fact that their foundations are floating on water.

Mississippi's casinos tend to be grouped primarily in three areas—the Gulf Coast (Biloxi, Gulfport, Bay St. Louis), Tunica (near Memphis), and Vicksburg. By far, the largest concentration of casinos is along the coast in Biloxi and Gulfport. Because these casinos are large and don't cruise, and because there are a number of them, here is where you'll find an experience most similar to Atlantic City and Las Vegas. All the games and slots are available and you can wander from casino to casino without too much difficulty.

Mississippi places no limits on bets or bankroll and it does not limit the number of casino licenses it is willing to issue. For this reason, Mississippi gaming was overbuilt for a while until the law of supply and demand asserted itself. As a result, some of the casinos didn't make it, while others prospered and expanded. Of all the new jurisdictions, I believe Mississippi casinos provide the most "user-friendly" environment. These unique casinos, which are staffed by friendly people skilled in Southern hospitality and free of hard-to-understand regulations, provide a fun experience for the gambler. If you have an opportunity to visit Mississippi, don't go home without visiting one of their unique floating gaming palaces—you'll be glad you did.

Missouri

Missouri law permits casino gaming on cruising riverboats. The boats must cruise, except for one landmark vessel in St. Louis which is exempt from cruising. This state had somewhat of a shaky start to legalized gaming. After it was approved by the voters, and after several casino operators built their boats, a court challenge resulted in prohibiting slot machines. It took months to get slot machines restored to these boats. As of this writing, the state maintains a $500-per-trip loss limit for customers, but Missouri still seems to be fine-tuning its rules regarding cruising, betting limits, and the like, so it would be a good idea to ask about the ground rules when you arrive to be certain you understand them. Nevertheless, many of the Missouri riverboats are beautiful, with elegant casinos worth a visit. Mark Twain would be proud to see these beauties once again gracing the river towns of his home state.

South Dakota

In South Dakota, the only legal casino gaming is in the old mining town of Deadwood—that's where Wild Bill Hickock was shot to death playing poker. (He was holding a pair of aces over a pair of eights, which, ever since, has been known as the "dead man's hand.")

When it comes to history and natural beauty, South Dakota's Black Hills are hard to beat and are worth the visit. Mount Rushmore is only a short drive from Deadwood. Unfortunately, Deadwood's casinos don't really merit a special trip, unless you live nearby and your options are limited. The casinos are rough and very small, each being limited to about thirty slot machines and a handful of blackjack and poker tables with $5 betting limits.

Comps? Not very likely here, but you might ask—if you can find a pit boss!

16

Those Exciting New Table Games

Red Dog, Caribbean Stud, and other exotic temptations

From time to time, I've been asked to explain some of the newer or less-well-known table games in a casino. Most of them are easy once you understand the concept, so don't let that old intimidation factor stop you from giving them a try. Even though you may not want to play them all the time, many of them are a fun way to pass the time or simply change the pace of your play for a little while. Here we go...

Sic Bo

Sic Bo (Big Small) is an ancient Chinese game played with three dice on a modern, electrically-lit table. The object of the game is for each player to pick individual numbers or combinations of numbers they think will appear after the three dice are shaken. The various possibilities and typical payoff schedules are:

One of a kind on one die	Pays 1	to 1
One of a kind on two dice	Pays 2	to 1
One of a kind on three dice	Pays 3	to 1
Two of a kind on a specific number	Pays 10	to 1
Three of a kind on a specific number	Pays 180	to 1
Three of a kind on any number	Pays 30	to 1
Any two-dice combination on specific numbers	Pays 5	to 1
Total value of 4	Pays 60	to 1
Total value of 5	Pays 30	to 1
Total value of 6	Pays 17	to 1
Total value of 7	Pays 12	to 1
Total value of 8	Pays 8	to 1
Total value of 9 thru 12	Pays 6	to 1
Total value of 13	Pays 8	to 1
Total value of 14	Pays 12	to 1
Total value of 15	Pays 17	to 1
Total value of 16	Pays 30	to 1
Total value of 17	Pays 60	to 1
"Big" (11–17)	Pays 1	to 1
"Small" (4–10)	Pays 1	to 1

To play Sic Bo, place your chips on the table layout directly on the numbers and/or combinations you want to bet on. Each player is responsible for positioning and keeping track of his or her own chips. After the dealer calls "No more bets," he or she will shake the dice that are sealed in a covered container. The shaker will be uncovered, revealing the dice and the dealer will enter the winning combinations into the electronic table layout. All winning combinations will be illuminated to show the winning bets. It's as easy as roulette or Big Six.

Red Dog

Red Dog is an easy, fast-paced game sometimes referred to as Ace-Deuce or Acey-Deucey. Here's how the game is played. The players each make a basic bet in the betting box in front of their position at the table. The dealer will deal two cards face up.

If the cards are:

Non-consecutive—you may raise your bet up to the amount of your original wager and a third card will be turned up. If the value of the third (middle) card is between the values of the other two cards, you will win up to five times your wager.

Consecutive—If there is no spread, and if the cards are not a pair, the hand is a tie. A third card is not drawn.

A pair—You may not raise your bet. However if the third card drawn makes three-of-a-kind, you have Red Dog! Three-of-a-kind wins eleven times your original bet. If the third card does not make three-of-a-kind, the hand is a tie.

Pai Gow Poker

Pai Gow Poker combines the ancient Chinese game if Pai Gow and the American game of Poker. Pai Gow Poker is played with one deck of 52 cards plus one joker. The joker can be used only as an Ace *or* to complete a Straight, a Flush, a Straight Flush or a Royal Flush.

In Pai Gow Poker, you have a chance to be the banker if you wish. If players have played a previous hand against the house banker, they will be allowed, if they wish, to bank the next game. In order for a player to bank, the player must have enough chips to cover all wagers made by the other players and the house. The house will normally wager an amount equal to the player's last bet against the house banker. The player banker may request the house to bet less or not at all. Likewise, if players have played a previous hand against the house banker, they will be allowed, if they wish, to co-bank with the house. The co-banker must have enough chips to cover one-half of the total wagers made by the other players; the house will cover the other half. The house will not have a wager while co-banking. The bank will be offered counter clockwise with the dealer banking in turn. If no player wishes to be banker, the dealer will always bank.

Once the bets are placed, the banker shakes a dice cup with three dice to determine to which player the dealer begins to deal the cards. Each betting area, including the dealer, is dealt seven cards. The players arrange their cards to make a two-card hand and a five-card hand. The five-card hand *must* be equal to or higher than the two-card hand. The hands are ranked in order of normal Poker hands.

The object of the game is to have both of the player's hands outrank both of the banker's hands. The banker will win all hands that rank exactly the same (a copy hand) as the player. If the player wins one hand but loses the other, it is a push. All winning hands are paid even money, less a 5 percent house commission. All casinos have set rules on how the house banker or player banker must set their hands. It would be best to ask if you play this game in a new or unfamiliar casino. The game sounds complicated, but, in reality, is quite simple and a lot of fun.

Caribbean Stud Poker

Caribbean Stud Poker is a new and exciting game that has achieved great popularity across the country and in the Caribbean (big surprise) as well. It offers something for everyone—beginners, high rollers and smaller bettors.

Caribbean Stud is a five-card stud poker game. To play, you make a bet in the ante box on the table layout in front of your seat. All ante bets must be made before the dealer calls "No more bets."

You will receive five cards face-down and the dealer will get four cards face down and one face-up. Once you have looked at your cards, you have the option of playing or folding. If you choose to play, you place a bet in the bet box exactly twice the amount of your ante bet. If you fold, you lose your ante bet.

After all players have made their decisions, the dealer then reveals his remaining four cards. If the dealer does not have an Ace and a King or higher in his hand, the dealer does not play and the player wins even money on the ante bet. No action is taken on the second bet and the hand is over.

If the dealer has an Ace and a King or higher, he plays his hand. He compares his hand with the players' cards (individually, right to left). If the player's hand beats the dealer's, then the player is paid even money on the ante bet and multiple odds on the second bet. The odds payout schedule is posted at the table. If the dealer and the player have the same hand, the remaining cards in the hand are taken into consideration and the highest hand wins. Suits are not counted. If all five cards are equal, the hand is considered a push.

In addition to table play in Caribbean Stud, there is an optional progressive jackpot feature. You play this by dropping one chip (the amount shown on the table) into the slot in the table in front of your betting box. This additional bet gives you the chance to win the amount on the progressive payout meter. Check with the pit boss or dealer for a further explanation of the progressive payouts.

Let It Ride

Let It Ride Poker is an enjoyable, easy-to-learn game that gives you an opportunity to control two of three bets on a unique, exciting poker-style game. It is based on five-card stud poker, but you do not play against the dealer or any other player.

To begin, each player places three equal bets in the circles labeled 1, 2, and 3. All bets must be placed at the beginning of the game before the dealer announces, "No more bets."

Each player and the dealer receives three cards face-down. You are not playing against the dealer or any other players. You are simply trying to get the best possible poker hand by using your three cards and the two community cards, which the dealer will expose. The winners are paid according to a payout schedule which ranges from even money for a pair of 10s or better, to 1,000 to 1 for a Royal Flush.

After looking at your first two cards, you may ask for your first bet back or "let it ride." The dealer, after burning his or her top card, turns up one community card. You may then ask for your second bet back or "let it ride." The dealer then turns up the second community card and, in a counterclockwise direction, turns the three cards of each player face up. After all losing wagers have been collected, the dealer pays all winning hands according to the payout schedule. Regardless of the decision you make on the first and second bets, you may not take back your third bet. Simple, huh?

Multiple Action Blackjack

A number of casinos now offer a "multiple action" form of Blackjack. Here are the rules for the multiple action game used at the Claridge in Atlantic City.

Basically this is a chance to get three times the action for your money. Multiple Action Blackjack allows players to play three rounds of Blackjack with a single hand against the dealer's first card, which is used for all three rounds of play. Each round is the same as one complete hand of regular Blackjack.

The game begins with players placing their bets in at least two of the three betting spots. Each player is dealt one card face up and the dealer receives one card face up in the first of the three squares in front of the chip rack. A second card is then dealt to each player. At this time, the dealer does not receive a second card.

Players now make their decision on how they will play their hand. Insurance will be offered if the dealer's card is an Ace. Players may double or split if they choose. The player's first hand and the dealer's first card will be used through all three rounds of play.

After all players have played their hands, the dealer completes his first hand by drawing one or more cards. The dealer then pays or picks up all first-round wagers. The dealer now picks up and discards only his hit card or cards, leaving his original card on the layout. Now the dealer's card is moved to the second square and the dealer completes his hand again. All second-round wagers are then paid or picked up. As after the first round, the dealer picks up and discards only his hit card or cards and leaves his original card on the layout. The dealer now moves his card to the third square and again completes his hand, paying or collecting all wagers at the conclusion of the round. All cards are then picked up and discarded and a new series of play will begin.

Obviously, there are other new games and are bound to be even more in the future. I hope my explanation of these games is helpful to you, but remember, in any well-run casino, the dealers and supervisors will always be more than happy to explain anything you don't understand. So, don't be afraid to ask.

17

Don't Go Home a Loser

You can and should improve your chances of winning!

Your education on "how to be treated like a high roller" is almost complete, except for a final bit of advice.

Getting treated like a high roller isn't what casino gambling is all about—*feeling* like a high roller is much more important. And, no surprise, the best way to feel like a high roller is to feel like a winner...to go home with more money than you started with.

Day after day, I hear people in the casino say, "Well, I've got a hundred bucks and when it's gone, it's gone. That's all I'm going to lose."

Does that sound like a good time? No, of course not!

But, tell the truth now...you've said it yourself, right?

The sad truth is that most people come to a casino expecting to lose. With that kind of an attitude, their expectations usually come true. But, just because most people lose, there's no reason for you to be one of them all the time. Be smart. There are things you can do and learn that will dramatically improve your chances of winning and minimize your chances of getting wiped out.

Here are some thoughts that may help you. I didn't invent them, but they're based upon common sense and are worth considering.

First of all, when you go to a casino, you should have a game plan. Decide in advance how much your bankroll will be and promise yourself not to lose more than half of it.

Furthermore, set a reasonable goal for how much you want to win. Notice I said *reasonable*. If your bankroll is $75, winning $100 is not a reasonable goal, $7.50 is. After all, that's a 10 percent profit in only a few hours. You'd probably move your savings account to another bank just to get another 1 percent per year. Don't be greedy, be realistic.

Next, don't risk your whole bankroll at one table in one session of play. Break it down into several equal amounts and play in shorter sessions with these "mini-bankrolls." If you lose half of your mini-bankroll at any session, quit and take a break. If you start to win, build your bankroll back up and then salt away at least half of your winnings without going back into it.

Play conservatively. Try to keep your individual bets fairly small so you can withstand a long losing streak and still be in action when the streak turns in your favor. Don't increase your bets unless you are winning. Players who increase their bets on a losing streak are called "steamers"—they only lose faster.

Learn the game you want to play as well as you can. Practice at home. Get a book about the game and develop some basic playing strategies that will keep you from giving the house a greater advantage than it already has.

If your point of view in the past has been that you'll probably lose but you just might get lucky, remember one thing. You can still get lucky when you're playing a smart, well-disciplined, conservative game…you're just less likely to get wiped out.

Your trips to a casino should be fun and exciting. Nobody has fun going home with empty pockets…feeling like a loser is a bad, bad feeling. It simply isn't necessary, and it's no fun, believe me.

There you have it. I hope you've enjoyed the book, and I really hope it helps you get more enjoyment and more profit out of your future casino visits.

Look me up if you get to Atlantic City—I'd like to meet you. Until then…

Good Luck!